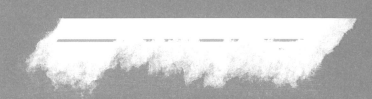

# PACIFIC PATTERN

# PACIFIC PATTERN

susanne küchler

graeme were

photographs by glenn jowitt

with 327 colour illustrations

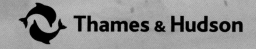
Thames & Hudson

Page 1: Maseiga Salua rolls pandanus leaves, Fusi, Upolu,
Samoa, 2003.
Page 2: A costume for the 2002 Miss Teuila Festival, made by
Vaasilii Fiti Moelgi Jackson, Apia, Samoa, 2002.
Page 3: New Guinea clansmen with bow and arrow, c. 1900.
Pages 4–5: New Guinea men's house. A thatched edifice
resembles a huge monster with jaws opening out towards
the sea – the place where spiritual forces emanate. Armed
men patrol the entrance, as only the initiated may enter.

First published in the United Kingdom in 2005 by Thames
& Hudson Ltd, 181A High Holborn, London WC1V 7QX

www.thamesandhudson.com

© Thames & Hudson Ltd, London
Text © 2005 Susanne Küchler and Graeme Were
Photographs taken by Glenn Jowitt © 2005 Glenn Jowitt

British Library Cataloguing-in-Publication Data
A catalogue record for this book is available from
the British Library

ISBN-13: 978-0-500-51237-1
ISBN-10: 0-500-51237-X

Printed and bound in Singapore by CS Graphics

# CONTENTS

# INTRODUCTION

Some of the most flamboyant designs of human imagination and skill have been expressed in the form of patterns. Nearly everything we see, use or wear features patterns of some kind or other. Most literature on the subject would have us suppose that the main function of such patterns is to make things beautiful, but they also have a fundamental role in structures and materials, especially fabrics, and thus bring the relation between textile and architecture into sharp relief. Nowhere is this more evident than in the Pacific, where patterns are woven, bound, knotted, plaited, rubbed or stamped using natural fibres from local plant resources. The raw materials used, such as the coconut palm or the leaves and the fruits of the pandanus palm, are richly symbolic of the renewal and the reproduction of life. These components are transformed into body wraps, walls and food containers, and the resulting patterns serve to translate temporal notions of heritage, history and memory into geometric forms which thereby come to carry ideas fundamental to society.

Patterns produced by fibres are the most neglected of all, largely because of their association with production processes that are carried out by women, but also because fibres often decay rapidly. It is, paradoxically, the ephemerality of fibre patterns that draws attention to ongoing design innovations in the Pacific as, unlike the dominant model in Europe or America, the value of their newness does not derive from contrast with age, nor with techniques of copying or restoration, but from a context of the constraints of production with transient materials, and of their impact on broader ideas of reproduction. The enduring nature of age-old patterns woven with synthetic packaging tape or plastic bags is, therefore, as much a hallmark of a hybrid, syncretic Pacific modernity as the more obvious use of introduced media.

The connection between fibre patterns and design innovation in the Pacific has been richly documented. For it was from here, during the eighteenth- and nineteenth-century era of European exploration, that vast quantities of fibre-based arts were systematically collected for museums and private collections in Europe, America and Australia. With the European textile industry reaching its heyday during this era, newly acquired designs from the Pacific gave entrepreneurs, aided by the creation of pattern books rich in the region's designs, the opportunity to diversify their products. At the same time, as European powers expanded into the Pacific, patterns used in Victorian clothing

Opposite: *Tivaivai* quilts hanging on a line to air. *Tivaivai* are sewn by women in Hawaii, Tahiti and the Cook Islands. It is uncertain exactly when quilting began in the Pacific, but we do know that missionary wives and Chinese sailors played an instrumental role in the introduction of quilting techniques. The quilts in the photograph are owned by the Rarotongan Beach Resort, Rarotonga, Cook Islands, which has been collecting *tivaivai* from local producers since the mid-1990s. The quilt designs, of types called *manu* and *ta taura*, are typical of the Cook Islands and show images of breadfruits, pineapples and flowers arranged symmetrically.

Below, left: Detail of a plaited coconut frond mat. In the Pacific, the leaves of the coconut palm are transformed into mats, baskets, hats and wall dividers.

Below, right: Salome Timothy weaves coconut fronds into a mat in Eton village, Efate, Vanuatu, 2004. The regular weave is offset by a contrasting pattern.

provided Pacific Islanders with focal points for technical innovation, resulting in a radical shift in traditional fibre-art production.

Yet the story of pattern in the Pacific remains largely untold, a symptom of its trivialization within the history of design. With its constellation of island communities dotted across the ocean expanse, the Pacific covers over one third of the world's surface area, but its total land mass excluding Australia equates to less than one eighth of that of Europe. Its expanse encompasses a vast region, bordered at the fringes by the islands of Hawaii to the north, Easter Island (Rapanui) to the east, and New Guinea to the southwest. The Pacific region is divided into three cultural zones – Melanesia, Polynesia and Micronesia – a colonial imposition that lumps island groupings together according

to shared cultural, historical and geographical traits. Despite the remoteness of some of these islands, the Pacific Islands are host to a complex diversity of peoples and languages, as well as some of the most imaginative and surreal artistic traditions known to humanity. Connections are made tangible through pattern, thereby enabling the flow of ideas, people and objects to overcome the obstacles set by the natural environment. In the increasingly diasporic reality in which many Pacific people find themselves, such tangible connections appear even more important than ever.

*Pacific Pattern* explores the arts from a diversity of island cultures well known for their prolific artistic practices, including those from Melanesia (Papua New Guinea, the Solomon Islands, Vanuatu, Fiji and New Caledonia), Polynesia (the Cook Islands, Tonga, Samoa, Niue, Tahiti, Hawaii and New

Below, left: Coconut palms standing on the shores of Efate, Vanuatu, 1997. The coconut palm is by far the most widespread and useful plant in the Pacific.

Below, right: Elsie Kaleb, a local weaver, stands with a freshly cut coconut palm leaf in Vorai village, Efate, Vanuatu, 2004.

Zealand, among others) and, when relevant, comparisons with Micronesian material. It sets out a history of patterns designed in fibre and fabric, the various techniques associated with fibre and fabric, and their cultural relevance to the people and their relationships to the societies in which the products are used and sold. Reaching beyond the well-described ritual domain to encompass pattern in the everyday sphere, this book captures the ideas inspired by baskets, mats, hats and fans made of coconut or pandanus fibre, for example, as well as the cut of cotton dresses, the openwork of crocheted tablecloths or stitched quilts, or even the openwork frames of fibre houses.

Indeed, pattern has assumed a pivotal place in Pacific modernity. We will argue that a new perspective on the role of pattern in the Pacific is given by considering the contrasting effects of lattice-work and cordage as technical processes offering alternative modes of visualizing cultural processes. Living kinds (bodies, places of habitation or the produce of garden or sea) are wrapped in a lattice of interlaced fronds in order to harness and protect the life contained within. 'Dead' things, or beings who live in proximity with the dead, on the other hand, are bound with cords whose tightening and unravelling activates the miracle of animation and of renewal. The designs of cordage works, typically used in rites of succession, are independent of the materials chosen and are largely conceptual. This way of fusing binding and thinking in the Pacific imagination has shaped the manner in which sewing techniques and clothing fashions have been appropriated by Pacific Islanders in the wake of colonialism and the introduction of Christianity.

## A Journey through History

We cannot understand the roles given to fibre patterns in the Pacific without first examining its people, their history, and the importance they invest in their social landscape and physical environment, such as the sea, sky and forests that are central features of their world. By describing this as a journey, we evoke a central theme of Pacific mythology and cosmology: Pacific Islanders recall their history through narratives of spatial and temporal movements of ancestors, or primeval beings, across the landscapes they reside in.

Almost all of the people, plants and animals found in the Pacific originated in Asia. According to archaeologists, the region was one of the last in which humans settled, with the first inhabitants of mainland New Guinea arriving from modern-day Indonesia some 40,000 to 50,000 years ago.

Opposite, above, left: Rolled pandanus leaves, Fusi, Upolu, Samoa, 2003. The spiky leaves of the pandanus palm are transformed through a series of treatments before they can be utilized for mat-making, hat-making or basketry. This generally involves stripping off the spikes, soaking the leaves in seawater, scraping and smoothing the leaves, as well as drying them.

Opposite, above, centre: Pandanus fruit, Efate, Vanuatu, 2004. The fruit of the pandanus is innovatively transformed into beautiful necklaces and headdress decorations as well as providing an instrument for painting designs on barkcloth.

Opposite, above, right: Pandanus plant, Apia, Samoa, 2003. The leaves of the pandanus are an important material for the production of patterned fibre art. There are numerous types of pandanus, distinguishable by their size and leaf shape, many of which, when dry, have distinctive colours, textures and material properties suitable for weaving.

Opposite, below: Detail of a pandanus mat, Mele village, Efate, Vanuatu, 2004.

Above, left: Barkcloth painting in Samoa, c. 1900. Women use the key of the pandanus plant to paint geometric designs on the surface of prepared barkcloth, beaten from the inner bark of the paper mulberry tree which grows across the Pacific.

Above, right: The beating of barkcloth over a wooden anvil in Samoa, c. 1900. The rhythmic sound of barkcloth beating echoes daily through Pacific villages, particularly in Tonga, Samoa and Fiji.

Below: Woven coconut leaf basket from the Marshall Islands, Micronesia. The design is reminiscent of a European needlework case, although it is woven using local materials and techniques.

These early migrations of (non-Austronesian) Papuan speakers involved crossing short distances between islands. This was made much easier by the lower sea level at that time, which reduced the distances between island groupings. These hunter-gatherers moved across the vast expanses of New Guinea before crossing into Australia via a land bridge at Cape York.

Around 5,000 years ago there were further dramatic changes. The inhabitants of New Guinea experienced a series of technological advances that enabled further migration eastwards across island archipelagos. New migrants from Southeast Asia, moving along the coastal regions of New Guinea, brought knowledge of agriculture and animal husbandry, as well as techniques for the construction of pottery and barkcloth (a fibrous cloth that is made from the inner bark of the paper mulberry tree). Crucially, they also brought new modes of transportation with them, most significantly the outrigger canoe, which enabled people to travel much greater distances across sea. There were migrations to the outlying New Guinea islands, to places such as New Britain, New Ireland and the Solomon Islands (together known as Island Melanesia). Migration continued further south-eastwards to Vanuatu (formerly known as the New Hebrides), Fiji and New Caledonia. Archaeological evidence suggests that these movements took place gradually over thousands of years and involved intermittent waves of small groups of people travelling by canoe.

The remains of pottery sherds and obsidian flakes support the claim that settlers arrived in island New Guinea and western Polynesia much later than central New Guinea and Australia. Archaeologists attribute these artefacts to the Lapita peoples, who inhabited a cultural zone that spreads across the Bismarck Archipelago region, parts of the New Guinea coastal region and into Fiji and western Polynesia. The Lapita peoples established trade networks, practised fishing and horticulture, and domesticated animals such as pigs. These cultural practices still resonate with life in the Pacific, to the extent that Lapita pottery has distinctive curvilinear motifs that bear close resemblance to twentieth-century tattooing and barkcloth designs. The Lapita peoples may well have also been the early pioneers of fibre-based patterns in the region, though the difficulty of finding archaeological evidence of such ephemeral products means that we may never know.

Some 3,500 years ago another phase in Pacific history unfolded, as the islands of eastern Polynesia were slowly colonized by people travelling by large outrigger canoe. Again, the movement of people across the region occurred slowly, often through navigating great distances between one island and the next – journeys in which many must have perished in the open sea. Migrants moved

Right: Woven pandanus leaf basket from Fiji. Pandanus leaves are cut and stripped of their spiny edges before being boiled and then dried. The leaves are blackened by burying them in mud and boiling them with special leaves in order to create darkened leaves for the manufacture of contrasting patterns.

Below: A 'native feast' in Hawaii, 1903. A group of men and women sitting on mats in front of a thatched building. The cooking and serving of food is a quintessential part of every gathering throughout the Pacific. The women in this picture are wearing loose missionary-style dress with flower garlands around their necks.

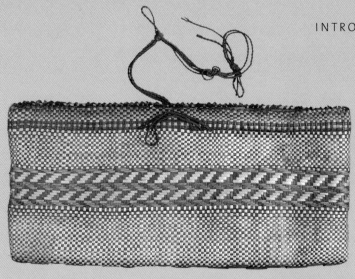

Above: Ceremonial exchange of red feather money, Santa Cruz, Solomon Islands, *c.* 1900. Feather money was used to settle ceremonial rights and obligations. It was made by specialists using tens of thousands of red feathers from the scarlet honeyeater bird.

Opposite: A Solomon Islander wearing woven sun-shade and shell ornaments, *c.* 1900.

from Tonga and Samoa to the Society Islands and Marquesas Islands. From here, they moved outwards towards Easter Island, then to the Hawaiian archipelago and finally towards New Zealand. These movements across the Pacific saw the colonization of the South Pacific by the descendants of the early migrants from Southeast Asia, and the birth of a complex of interrelated cultures. These people pushing into the eastern Pacific spoke Austronesian languages (formerly known as Malayo-Polynesian) and were therefore distinct from the early people of New Guinea and the Bismarck Archipelago, who were Papuan speakers.

The next major phase in the history of the Pacific began about 500 years ago with the arrival of the first Europeans. The early encounters were generally with passing ships, and it was not until the eighteenth and nineteenth centuries that Europeans – with improved navigational techniques, growing colonial ambitions and an eagerness to exploit the region's natural resources – established longer-lasting relationships. Traders, explorers and whalers were some of the first European peoples to have frequent, sustained contact in the region, and many of them established trading posts in the Pacific Islands. European settlers colonized Australia and New Zealand first, partly because the environments were much like those in Europe; in contrast, the tropical climates of New Guinea and the Solomon Islands were far less hospitable and European settlement was considerably less appealing. By the end of the nineteenth century, the British, French, German, Dutch and Americans had established colonies throughout the South Pacific. The Japanese also controlled a part of the region, an area that increased during the Second World War, before the loss of Japan's colonial territories with their surrender in 1945.

At the same time that governments were setting up administrative bureaucracies to control the local people and pacify the region, waves of evangelical missionaries were streaming into the area with the aim of converting the Pacific Islanders to Christianity. This period of intense missionary activity – which began around the 1790s and lasted until the 1930s – has had a major impact on the region, leaving visible traces on current religious thinking, art styles and clothing fashions.

Today, Christianity dominates religious worship across the South Pacific. Virtually every islander belongs to one denomination or another, and the church is a central concern in people's lives. Even though it is tempting to assume that Christianity homogenized religious practices and enforced conformity, there still exist strong commitments to traditional values and beliefs, which are currently undergoing a rebirth in contemporary Pacific society. As we shall see, both rural and urban life revolve

Above: Women rolling freshly made barkcloth in Mua village, Tongatapu, Tonga, 2003. Barkcloth is made by groups of women.

Opposite, above: Tools of the trade, Mua village, Tongatapu, Tonga, 2003. Barkcloth-making tools arranged on a wooden anvil, featuring three wooden beaters, two strips of unrolled barkcloth and rolls of freshly beaten bark.

around the social activities organized by the church: from religious celebrations such as Easter parades to fundraising events in local villages. It is during these gatherings that women sit in groups, avidly making a variety of fibre arts for spectacular performances involving colourful costumes and decorations.

## Plants and their Uses: Coconut, Pandanus and Barkcloth

When we think of Pacific art, we immediately envisage exotic images of carved wooden objects, intricately incised shell ornaments and a range of weaponry such as spears and axes. These objects feature predominately in the largely male domain of ritual and preoccupy art historians and

Bottom row, left: 'Samoan petty chief and his attendants', all in barkcloth wraps, c. 1900. The seated man's chiefly status is denoted by his fly whisk of coconut fibres.

Centre: Middle-aged woman on a pandanus mat in Tonga, c. 1900.

Right: Man in front of a thatched house with woven coconut palm leaf walls in Samoa, c. 1900.

Below, left: Fijian dancers wearing Fijian barkcloth (*masi*) patterned with stencilled designs at the 7th Festival of Pacific Arts, Apia, Samoa, 1996. The man on the left clutches a traditional wooden club carved from hardwood.

Below, right: Young man wearing Samoan barkcloth, Apia, Samoa, 2003.

anthropologists concerned with the interrelation between art and religion. The resulting fetishization of these objects often obscures significant differences between religious beliefs in Polynesia and Melanesia. Generally speaking, Polynesians hold a belief in gods that are able to occupy carved, woven or wrapped objects. Ritual objects, such as woven gods or barkcloth, are imbued with *mana* – ancestral power, which is deemed to come from the gods. In Melanesia, in contrast, religious beliefs centre on the worship of ancestors. Many religious activities stem from a desire to secure access to the resources and benefits enjoyed by those deceased who have entered into the ancestral domain. Made of wood, bark and plant materials, artworks created in Melanesia draw on aspects of landscapes in which ancestral powers are believed to reside, and they are typically displayed during

highly charged performances in which groups of people gather to participate. In Polynesia, likewise, many artworks, prior to the introduction of cloth and Christianity, were created from feathers and fibres, as well as wood and shell. Today, most objects for ceremonial purposes are made from vegetable fibres and cloth. Despite differing emphases on inherited or achieved forms of authority, both regions defined rank and status with relation to control of imagery associated with elaborate competitive exchanges.

The technical expertise employed in the production of the better-known (to Western collectors) wood carvings in the Pacific is also utilized in the creation of fibre and fabric patterns, especially in the use of the coconut palm and the pandanus palm and in the production of barkcloth. As we shall

Below, left: Matai (chief) Tuitova'a Siaso wearing Samoan-style barkcloth, Apia, Samoa, 2003.

Below, right: Tongan dancers from Tonga College at the 85th birthday of King Tupou IV, Tonga, 2003. The designs are stencilled with *kupesi* design boards, before freehand motifs are added in black ink with the key of the pandanus plant.

see, the way Pacific Islanders transform coconut and pandanus leaves, and the bark of the paper mulberry tree, both suggests a common history and, at the same time, distinguishes social groups and island identities.

The coconut is the seed of the coconut palm and it grows where it falls. Thus, in the same way that seafaring groups populated the Pacific Islands, coconuts are washed up, the palms sprout and grow along the high tidemarks of the islands, making the coconut iconic of the renewal of life. The coconut palm is by far the most widespread and useful plant in the Pacific. Coconut oil is often rubbed on the skin or hair and has medicinal properties. Coconut milk quenches the thirst, while the white interior flesh is a staple food. The exterior husk is commonly used as kindling to light fires, but it can also be utilized for making string or for weaving. The trunk, meanwhile, is used in house building,

as well as in the construction of canoes. Many Pacific Islanders realize the commercial potential of coconut palms by growing them on small plantations in order to earn money from a cash-crop, copra, the dried coconut kernels from which oil is extracted. Producing copra involves removing the fleshy white interior of the coconut and drying it in a special oven, before packing it in sacks for export.

The nut and trunk are far from the only parts of this amazing tree used in the Pacific. Islanders cut down its leaves and transform them into an array of baskets, mats, fans, cooking containers and screens within houses. The leaves are large, sometimes measuring up to six metres in length. In northern New Ireland, for example, coconut leaves are woven into an array of different-shaped baskets: large ones are designed to carry loads of root vegetables, while smaller ones are simply used to carry personal possessions. Coconut leaves are also used to make a diverse array of headwear. In the Cook Islands, for example, the more flexible inner leaves are used as an ideal medium for weaving delicate hats, known as *rito*, which are often decorated with coloured beads or seashells. At festivals, quickly made hats (such as those overleaf) provide protection from the sun, while individual flowers are threaded on to plaited coconut palm fronds to create head leis, garlands of flowers (seen in the examples above).

The leaves of the pandanus palm, which grows largely uncultivated across the Pacific Islands, are another important material for the production of patterned fibre art. However, in some islands, especially the Cook Islands and Tonga, they are also cultivated in groves close to the houses of people who use the leaves for weaving. Weavers can identify numerous types of pandanus by their varying colours, sizes and leaf shapes, many of which, when dry, have distinctive colours, textures and material properties suitable for weaving.

In the Cook Islands, as in other areas of the Pacific, women weave pandanus leaves together to make colourful sleeping mats. A cluster of leaves are dried and then rolled into a large coil. They are stored like this until they are required for use in mat-making. Women also weave pandanus purses that incorporate bright patterns of dyed hibiscus fibres, plaited horizontally through the pandanus weaves. In Niue, and in some parts of Vanuatu, women weave baskets out of dried pandanus leaves. The baskets create a visual openwork effect that islanders recognize as coming from specific island communities.

Arguably, the most famous and distinctive medium for Pacific fibre arts is barkcloth, a type of fibrous material deriving from the bark of the paper mulberry tree. Barkcloth, more commonly known as *tapa*, is found across the breadth of Polynesia as well as in some parts of Melanesia, including Papua New Guinea. In Tonga, Fiji and Samoa, the tradition of making barkcloth remains strong.

Opposite: Kaena Mataiapo Tutara receiving the title of Warrior Chief at a ceremony in Arorangi village, Rarotonga, Cook Islands, 1998. Hereditary chiefly titles still pertain today in the hierarchically structured societies of Polynesia, whereas in Melanesia – particularly in Papua New Guinea – positions of rank are acquired through the ability to organize competitive gift exchanges.

Above, left: Girl wearing head lei (flower headband), a garland of flowers, at the Pasifika Festival in Auckland, New Zealand, 2004. In Polynesia, the wearing of flower head decorations is a necessary part of everyday clothing accessories for married women and is a quintessential decorative accessory worn during festivities for younger girls. Flowers are chosen for their scent and colour and may be cultivated close to the house for the purpose of accessibility.

Above, right: Woman wearing head lei (flower headband) at the 2003 Tiare (Flower) Festival on the island of Rarotonga, Cook Islands, which takes place every year in November. The flower lei is constructed from a plaited coconut palm frond on which individual flowers are threaded.

Left: Women shielding their heads from the sun with quickly made coconut palm frond hats at the Teuila Festival, Apia, Samoa, 2003.

Above: Quickly made basket woven from coconut fronds by Tokerau Munro on the island of Rarotonga, Cook Islands, 2003.

Opposite: Man wearing 'quick' coconut frond hat and a pandanus necklace at the Teuila Festival, Apia, Samoa, 2003.

Overleaf, clockwise from top left: Detail of a dance costume made for the Miss Tonga competition, Mua, Tongatapu, Tonga, 2003; Miss Tonga contestant performing at the Heilala Festival, Nuku'alofa, Tonga, 2003; detail of a dance costume made for the Miss Tonga competition, Mua, Tongatapu, Tonga, 2003; Winnie Moala making a dance dress for the Miss Tonga competition using pandanus seeds and white polystyrene, Mua, Tongatapu, Tonga, 2003.

Barkcloth is still a high-prestige object used within ceremonial exchanges in contemporary Pacific life, although it is no longer produced in many places largely owing to missionary influences.

To make barkcloth, the paper mulberry tree is cultivated to a height of around two metres. Women then strip the bark from the trunk, clean it, and leave it in the sun to dry before soaking it overnight. The soaked bark is beaten on a wooden anvil with a special implement resembling a mallet until the bark forms a fibrous material. The strips are then joined by beating them together in a criss-cross formation in order to create a thick and quite rigid piece of cloth. In Tonga, patterns are rubbed on to the surface of the barkcloth using a fragile stencil, while in Niue women apply motifs freehand. Size, texture and patterning are important elements and are indicative of provenance and ritual value.

By closely examining the way these natural materials are ingeniously transformed into patterned baskets, mats, hats and other fibre arts, we can begin to understand the rich diversity in design innovation that exists across the Pacific. Furthermore, in tracing the technical means by which their patterns are engineered, we may see the process of their creation not just as a functional attribute of the design of an object, but rather as an intellectual activity designed to manage relations both temporally and spatially. It is from this perspective that this book develops.

Opposite: Sakaria Toetu with decorated bicycle using *teuila* flowers for the parade at the Teuila Festival, Apia, Samoa, 2003. The bright red colour of the floral decoration is carefully coordinated with the cyclist's clothing, including a garland of flowers and a hat as accessories, giving an overwhelming sense of vitality. Red is still associated with chiefly status in Polynesian culture and may be chosen here to draw attention to prosperity.

Above: Bridge decoration using the midrib of the coconut palm frond and hibiscus flowers, Upolu, Samoa, 2003.

# A HISTORY
# OF PATTERN
# IN FIBRE
# AND FABRIC
# IN THE
# SOUTH PACIFIC

# 1

Preceding pages: Matautia Ieriko
Niulevaea and Matautia Peni
wait to be given their chiefly
Matai titles, Utufa'alalafa,
Upolu, Samoa, 2003.

Above, left: 'Natives at Pago Pago,
Savo', the Solomon Islands, 1906.
The men wear traditional face
paint with European cloth
garments, some of which feature
decorative motifs and patterns.

Above, right: 'Vila harbour, Efate,
New Hebrides', Vanuatu, 1906.
Large bays, where ships could
easily navigate and anchor,
became the epicentre for trade
and missionary enterprises during
the colonization of the Pacific.
Towns or large villages sprung up
in the vicinity as a consequence.

Opposite, left: New Guinean
men working on a plantation
with mission station in the
background, c. 1900.

Opposite, right: Missionary
wife posing with New Guinean
converts, dressed in matching
outfits. Missionaries viewed
the adoption of dress as evidence
of conversion to Christianity.
The choice of the pattern and
the modification of the dress also
carried forward traditional ideas.

Background: 'Coast, Steep Cliff
Bay, Pentecost, New Hebrides',
Vanuatu, 1906. Europeans
were often greeted on the beaches,
where exchanges of provisions
for cloth, scrap metal and weapons
took place.

European colonization of the Pacific decisively shaped the arts of the region. Over the past two centuries, from the time of the first European settlement, some artistic practices have gradually sunk into decline, while other modes of visual and material expression, such as fibre arts, have flourished through the innovative adoption of European materials and resources. Indeed, given the eminent usefulness of many fibre arts, their embedment in technology and their intimate role in everyday life, one would be surprised if such designs had disappeared with the arrival of fabric, plastic containers and European furniture.

Fibre arts have not just managed to endure change in the Pacific – they have become the tangible and yet fragile cloak for new ideas and social relations. In contrast to ritual items, which were debased on a grand scale by missionaries, the very practicality of many fibre arts averted adverse suspicion. In some areas, such as Tonga and across eastern Polynesia, fibre arts filled the void of the prohibited ritual objects. As a result, they took on heightened significance as carriers of socially relevant ideas to a wider audience. Ironically, in parts of the Pacific, missionaries who saw fibre arts as an appropriate pastime for women ended up contributing to a thriving ritual economy – a situation that largely escaped their attention. This ritual economy manifested itself in the production and exchange of fibre arts using traditional media and introduced fabrics.

These factors not only indicate why fibre arts thrive today, but also why fibre-based technologies lie at the root of much innovation in Pacific art. The perspective they give enables us to begin making connections between otherwise disparate objects. So, for example, we can explore links between patterned barkcloth and brightly patterned quilts in the Cook Islands; or fibrous leaf body decorations and island-specific patterned

ankle-length flowing dresses in Vanuatu; or woven ceremonial aprons and string figures with crocheted waist coverings in Tonga. The history of fibre arts in fact details how Pacific Islanders dealt with change: for transformations of the thread, the frond and the strip not only capture the contemporary arts of the Pacific, but they also reveal how islanders have successfully adapted to new social relations and ways of doing things.

## European Exploration and Stereotypes

The earliest contacts Europeans had with Pacific Islanders were in the sixteenth century, when ships voyaging around the South Pacific made sightings of land and people, although no significant economic exchanges took place. Dealings with islanders were only intermittent up until the eighteenth century, when a more systematic exploration of the region began in earnest, driven by economic desire. In an entrepreneurial spirit, whalers and merchants travelling out across the island archipelagos made sustained contacts with Pacific people. On many islands European sailors set up trading bases, where they could drop anchor and exchange hoop-iron, strips of cloth and discarded clothing for such items as food supplies, sandalwood, turtle-shell and local arts and crafts.

In Europe, rumours abounded about the practices of Pacific Islanders, and a stereotype quickly emerged which mapped ideological distinctions of races on to the geographic division of the Pacific into Melanesia, Polynesia and Micronesia. Europeans considered the people of the Polynesian Islands to be friendly and hospitable, tall, chiefly and noble, and their elaborate mythologies allowed them to be likened to the ancient Greeks;

Above: Opening ceremony of the 8th Festival of Pacific Arts, Noumea, New Caledonia, 2000, performed by New Caledonian dancers. Ground coral as a base is mixed with the water of the green coconut and used as a temporary body decoration across Island Melanesia, a region that separates the mainland of Papua New Guinea from the Polynesian Islands to the east. Fibrous skirts and head decorations animate and accentuate the leg, arm and head movements of the dancers.

Opposite: Dancers from New Caledonia at the 7th Festival of Pacific Arts, Apia, Samoa, 1996.

Overleaf, left: 'Kapkap' shell valuable from New Ireland, Papua New Guinea. Victorian collectors took special delight in amassing large collections of this striking shell ornament made of turtle-shell fretwork overlaying a clamshell disc. Its portability, its affinity to medals and its intricate craftsmanship ensured its popularity.

The image in the background shows Papuan Gulf clansmen carrying patterned shields, c. 1900. Decorative artefacts such as these were collected en masse in the late nineteenth and early twentieth centuries. Social evolutionary theories fashionable at this time considered such designs as indicative of non-complex societies, and they were therefore classified as 'primitive' in nature.

in marked contrast, the people of Melanesia were depicted as violent, dangerous and savage barbarians because they reputedly practised headhunting and cannibalism. These contrasting visions fuelled the perceptions and the fears of many European sailors voyaging to the South Pacific, while at the same time stimulating the interest of people back home in Europe and America.

Apprehension towards Melanesians was so great that European traders and explorers often refrained from setting foot on their islands, preferring instead to barter with local people from the relative safety of their ships, which were anchored just off shore. Stories about sailors and missionaries who had been brutally attacked or cannibalized meant that Europeans rarely ventured into the forested interiors of the islands.

In contrast, sailors visiting the islands of Polynesia reported an aura of sexual licentiousness. The stereotypical image of dark-haired women paddling out on canoes to greet the European sailors in their ships persists even today. The chiefly nobility of the islands often received European visitors as honoured guests and, in places such as Hawaii and Tahiti, local dignitaries quickly adopted European habits and dress in an attempt to reinforce the existing hierarchical order of society.

Unfortunately, as in other places that experienced European colonization, the influx of Europeans brought new diseases to which the indigenous population was unaccustomed. Illnesses such as influenza, smallpox and venereal disease swept across the region, causing massive declines in the populations of many islands.

## Collecting in the Pacific

European expansion into the South Pacific in the nineteenth century coincided with the heyday of collecting, when vast quantities of arts and crafts such as sculptures and shell valuables were systematically shipped back from across the world to meet the demands of Western museums and private collections. Nineteenth-century European society shared an avid interest in the exploits of the explorers and traders navigating the world, who often brought back tales of their adventures with exotic people in distant lands. The arts and crafts they took with them, which became regarded as 'curiosities', were the closest

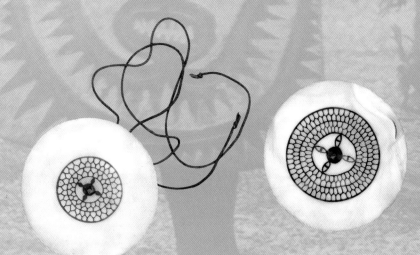

Left: European man seated with two Tongan women dressed in part European and part traditional fibre clothing, c. 1900.

Right: Maori male ritual figure from New Zealand, mid-19th century. This naturalistic figure represents an important Maori ancestor and would once have been found inside the sacred space of a Maori meeting house.

Right: 'Kapkap' shell valuable from New Ireland, Papua New Guinea. This type of striking shell ornament was favoured by Victorian collectors, who built up large collections of such items.

Below: Six Polynesian women on board a ship dressed in pandanus mats, fabric blouses, head garlands and cloth neck decorations, c. 1900.

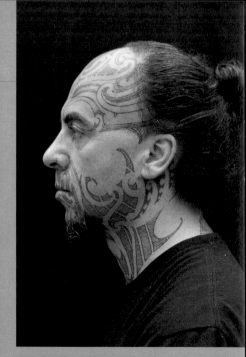

Portrait of a Maori facial tattoo called Moko by Haki Williams, Laingholm, Auckland, New Zealand, 2004. Maori full body tattooing has the double effect of containing and shielding the potentially harmful effects of *tapu*, an invisible life force which resides in darkness and can emanate through bodily orifices.

Opposite: Back tattoo. Upper back by Haki Williams and lower back by Gordon Toi, Laingholm, Auckland, New Zealand, 2004.

Clockwise, from top left: Shell disc earplug with incised pattern from the Solomon Islands; shell-inlaid wooden container from Palau, Micronesia, nineteenth century; detail of Marquesas Island club; painted wooden shield, Papuan Gulf.

Background: Tongan women wrapped in cloth, c. 1900.

most Europeans came to Pacific Islanders. These artefacts provoked a stream of debates concerning the origins of Pacific peoples and their relationship to European civilization in evolutionary history. This led to the justification of the ever-increasing numbers of expeditions to the region. Curiosities from the Pacific legitimized the work of missionaries and reinforced the categorical distinction between religious piety on the one hand and paganism on the other.

By the late nineteenth century, ethnographic museums were being founded on the hoards of objects collected from trade and scientific expeditions around the world. Every conceivable kind of artefact was collected: from ritual paraphernalia – such as ornate barkcloth masks for funerary rites – to the mundane cooking utensil. Fibre arts, although fragile, were often highly portable, and were thus represented in large quantities in European and American museums. Once the museums were established, one of the overt reasons for continuing to collect was the belief that these artefacts should be salvaged as quickly as possible, before European civilization ravaged and finally destroyed the Pacific way of life.

In the twentieth century, the collection process formed part of an emerging scientific programme of enquiry into the origins of human civilization in which artefacts were treated as scientific specimens. Once in Europe, these objects were catalogued, numbered and arranged according to curators' perceptions of their place in an evolutionary scale (comparable to the Linnaean classification of animals and plants formed by Swedish botanist Carl Linnaeus in the eighteenth century).

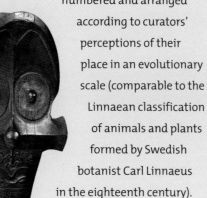

As the anthropologist Nicholas Thomas argues, objects from the Pacific were abstracted from their natural context and aligned, side-by-side, as though they were natural specimens ready to be studied. This process of abstraction – the way in which the objects were divorced from their original context to be placed in a theoretical one – was formative of the Victorian style of museum exhibition, in which rows upon rows of objects were displayed without any reference to peoples.

It is important to point out that for Western scholars these curiosities were material manifestations of a primal state in which the Pacific peoples were generally thought to live. In effect, the curiosities collected by Europeans were used to support the dominant view of Western superiority over the 'noble savage'. A huge variety of objects – clubs and shields, masks and figures, decorative fibrous strips of coconut and pandanus fronds – were construed to reinforce notions of 'primitive' technology, religion and design.

Social theorists seized on Pacific patterns, whose features offered themselves to simple classification in a schema grading the complex and the non-complex. Arguably the most famous work to examine Pacific art, *Evolution in Art* (1895) by the British anthropologist and museum curator Alfred Cort Haddon, laid out a methodical study of decorative art traditions as though they were biological specimens. In it he states that, 'the decorative art of a particular region has been studied much in the same way as a zoologist would study a group of its fauna, say the birds or butterflies'. For him, the decorative arts of the Pacific presented a vital clue to the origins of European civilization, 'All we can do is to study the art of the most backward peoples, in the hope of gaining sufficient light to cast a glimmer down the gloomy perspective of the past'. Geometric ornamentation, Haddon believed, was a symptom of non-complex societies and would therefore appear at the lower end of the evolutionary scale. Elaborate forms of ornamentation, such as those found in European art and architecture, were considered to be characteristic of sophisticated societies and would therefore rank highly.

Yet with prolonged European contact in the Pacific and elsewhere, the classification of decorative art into that of complex and non-complex societies became problematic.

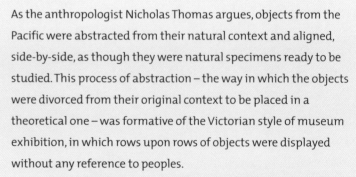

Inevitably, with European intervention in such places as Africa, North America and the Pacific, local artistic practices began to change, often in relation to the increased availability of European goods. European design systems and materials inspired local artists and offered new challenges. However, curators and private collectors interested in amassing vast hoards of Pacific curiosities considered objects displaying signs of innovation to be inauthentic.

Twenty-first-century collections still bear the hallmarks of nineteenth-century European ideals, when the decorative arts were associated with strong moral ideas. According to nineteenth-century designer and architect Owen Jones, pattern systems from 'primitive' societies were pure and untainted (as an example he used the curvilinear forms of Maori tattooing and figurative carving), while European designs risked corruption and overindulgence. These perceptions were shared by museum curators and collectors: what was crucial for them was that Pacific designs appeared free from European influence. Collections took shape on the basis that objects remained true to their 'traditional' form; artefacts that showed signs of change were systematically ignored. Perceptions of inauthenticity in designs were expressed in terms of corruption, taintedness or alteration. Stylistic integrity and natural materials were regarded as markers of authenticity, while metals, cloth and anything bearing a resemblance to Western forms were generally rejected. These preoccupations with authentic design systems persist with many modern Western collectors. Many Western museums still subscribe to policies of acquiring 'traditional' objects rather than those displaying signs of European influence, and the Pacific art we see on display today is largely that of the nineteenth and early twentieth centuries.

To the Victorian curator of the then new collections of Pacific artefacts, the great diversity of their designs might have appeared at odds with the primitive position assigned to the region, as they might well have reminded them of the similar diversity found in the catalogues of late nineteenth-century mail-order companies, department stores and manufacturers, which offered dazzling choices of everything from pens to sewing machines and dining-room chairs. These designs fell into distinct categories that generally corresponded to social boundaries and distinctions, from high society to the very mundane. Yet while ritual and high status designs attracted increasing attention as a way of understanding the societies of the newly charted Pacific, the significance of the diversity of designs in everyday fibre products was overlooked.

It is thus not surprising that the arrays of basketry, fans and mats that found their way into Europe were hardly mentioned in the literature. The disregard of fibre collections is apparent when contrasted with the detailed documentation afforded to virtually every other aspect of society. The earliest documented collections of fibre artefacts were gathered during Captain James Cook's three voyages between 1768 and 1780. As with later explorers, Cook and his men brought back baskets from the Pacific that were given to them, or that appealed to them, with as much care as a tourist choosing a souvenir – without caring to note down the basis on which they were chosen, and without providing such information as source, use, technique or exact origin. 'Early explorers and scientists', as the basketry expert Wendy Arbeit puts it, 'rarely described the baskets they saw, surely in great variety. The plain baskets most typical of a culture were ignored altogether.'

Above, from left to right: Hymn book, fan and reading glasses left on a church pew in Mauke, Cook Islands, 1991; Church of St Louis, Fusi, Samoa, 1996; Church of the Sacred Heart, Upolu, Samoa, 1996.

Below: Avarua Cook Island Christian Church during a Sunday service, Avarua, Rarotonga, Cook Islands, 1991.

Right, from left to right: Tongan bride wearing European-style wedding dress, *c.* 1900; woman wearing fine mat, girdle and headdress in Samoa, *c.* 1900; King George Tupou II of Tonga, *c.* 1900, wearing European suit; studio portrait of Tongan Crown Prince posing in a Western-style suit with fob watch, *c.* 1900.

# New Ideas, Materials and Techniques

With European expansion into the Pacific, an influx of new materials and resources became available through the trade between islanders and Europeans. Materials such as trade calico (cloth), old clothing, hoop-iron, newspapers, army surplus such as rifles, hats and belts, and prized glass trade-beads and whales' teeth appeared in abundance in the region and were traded for local arts and crafts, sandalwood, turtle-shell and food essentials.

The importing of second-hand European cloth and clothing had a great impact on the fibre arts of the Pacific. Pacific women quickly recognized the potential contained within their fibrous textures: cloth and clothing could easily be cut and re-stitched to resemble the patterns made by weaving coconut fronds, pandanus leaves and printing barkcloth. Much cloth and clothing was unpicked and transformed into such items as net bags, baskets or body decorations. Other imported materials, such as metal axe blades, were also seized upon by Pacific Islanders and replaced traditional stone and wooden tools. These metal tools – stronger and more efficient – liberated the work that went into the production of arts and crafts, leading to changes in techniques.

The wide-scale conversion to Christianity in the region – one of the most profound transformations in Pacific history – acted as a driving force behind such changes. Once firm contacts with Pacific Islanders became established, evangelical missionaries poured into the region. The peak of this missionary activity – from the late eighteenth to the early twentieth century – coincided with the period of intense collecting, when missionaries from England, Germany, France and North America set up bases all over Polynesia and, later, Melanesia.

Missionaries were responsible for dramatically changing the religious practices, artistic traditions and social landscape of the Pacific. There were many positive implications of their interventions: in particular, missionaries can be credited with setting up schools in local communities and offering a basic education to the children of converts. Regimes of health and sanitation, in which villagers were inspected regularly for levels of cleanliness and signs of disease, were introduced into rural villages. Larger mission stations built clinics so that local people could receive medical attention, though more often than not only Christian converts could receive treatment.

Missionaries particularly disapproved of traditional religious practices, mistakenly likening them to devil worship. In many places missionaries enforced Christian values in draconian fashion and attempted to ostracize those maintaining traditional religious practices. Often, converts caught participating in 'heathen' practices were punished. Dancing and carving were especially despised, and in some regions of the Pacific they were even forbidden. Carved wooden objects, ceremonial masks and other ritual paraphernalia were often burnt, sometimes as a spectacle in full view of the village community – in an attempt to demonstrate that they contained no supernatural power and that no retribution ensued. It is documented that local converts were often complicit in these acts of iconoclasm, helping missionaries in the collection and destruction of many objects. Other items were simply confiscated, with thousands being sent to Europe as demonstrations of the good work of the missions.

Arguably the most visible of the transformations brought about by missionaries was the introduction of European dress to the South Pacific, along with the modes of deportment and

domesticity associated with wearing clothes. At first, cloth and clothing were scarce, though missionaries quickly recognized the need to clothe Pacific Islanders. From the late nineteenth century onwards, the distribution of discarded Victorian clothing became a high priority though, as photographic records depict, many Pacific Islanders adopted European dress idiosyncratically. For instance, photographs capture men from the Solomon Islands wearing European patterned cloth as neckerchiefs, or women in Tikopia wearing European petticoats underneath their traditional grass skirts. Conversely, in other parts of the Pacific, in areas such as Hawaii, the Cook Islands, Fiji and Samoa, barkcloth clothing was invented to mimic European dress.

The adoption of clothing became an important sign of a person's conversion to Christianity and provided visual evidence of successful efforts to proselytize sometimes indifferent populations. Missionaries believed that a clothed body was closer to God than a naked one, so when Pacific Islanders adopted European modes of dress the missionaries thought they were taking their first steps towards accepting the teachings of the Bible. At the same time, missionaries were wary of undue attention being paid to clothing, as this might distract converts from achieving the salvation believed to be located in the Word alone.

Many, mainly evangelical, missionary organizations targeted the Pacific. Of these, the most sustained interventions came from the London Missionary Society and the Wesleyan Methodist Missionary Society. However, other missionary organizations, such as the French Catholic Marists and German Sacred Heart Brothers, also claimed significant ground across the Pacific, often in direct competition with each other over the hearts and minds of the local people. The London Missionary Society is perhaps the most famous missionary organization to establish itself in the Pacific. The society was formed in the late eighteenth century during the revival of Protestant Evangelism with the specific aim of spreading the knowledge of Christ to places adhering to pagan beliefs and practices. Their missionary activity initially concentrated on the Pacific, with the first mission station set up in Tahiti in 1796, and soon expanded across the Cook Islands to Samoa. Their technique of conversion often involved deployment of Polynesian converts as teachers of the new faith.

The Wesleyan Methodist Missionary Society was also founded in the late eighteenth century and in a similar fashion, with the same aims of proselytizing the faith to non-Christians. One of the most famous Methodist missionaries was George Brown, who established a base in New Britain (Papua New Guinea) in 1875. He set out to convert villages along the coastline of New Britain and the adjacent island of New Ireland with the aid of Polynesian missionaries.

Although the introduction of European clothing went hand-in-hand with mission Christianity, we should not assume that Pacific Islanders were passive recipients of missionary teachings. On the contrary, we can see from the rich historical information in museum collections, missionary diaries and ethnographic photographs that much European clothing was transformed into locally specific styles. Sometimes it was hidden away from sight and revealed for ceremonial exchange, or radically altered in a way that made the original garment almost unrecognizable. Clothing was, in fact, taken up in a strategic fashion, with Pacific Islanders perceiving dress as a radically new resource for the expression of novel modes of being and thinking.

Opposite: Dancers wearing traditional costumes and coconut bras at the Heiva Festival, Papeete, Tahiti, French Polynesia, 1999.

Above, top: Dancers performing at the banana festival, Poue'bo, New Caledonia, 2000.

Above, bottom: Male dancer at the Heiva Festival, Papeete, Tahiti, French Polynesia, 1999. The Heiva Rima'i is organized annually by the Ministry of Arts and Crafts in Tahiti.

Novel transformations become apparent when we examine how the new resources brought into the region by missionaries were used. For instance, many Pacific women enrolled in sewing classes run by the wives of missionaries. In places such as the Cook Islands, sewing liberated the women from the arduous work that went into the production of barkcloth garments for ceremonial exchange, and led to the development of new clothing styles. Large, elaborate appliqué quilts began to be made in eastern Polynesia where, as we discuss later, barkcloth techniques were abandoned for technologies used in layered quilting, fuelled by the emphasis placed on stitch and line.

## Colonialism, Independence and Diaspora

Colonialism also left its mark on the fibre arts of the Pacific. During the late nineteenth century almost all Pacific people lived under some form of colonial rule – most until the last quarter of the twentieth century – although the colonial governments were, on the whole, non-interventionist. Today, islanders celebrate independence through a whole host of events, including pageants, parades and performances.

New Guinea, the largest island in the Pacific, was divided between Germany (the north-eastern part), Britain (the south-eastern part) and the Netherlands (the western half) in 1885. In 1902, the British transferred their portion to Australia, and after the First World War the north-eastern part also fell under Australian administration, with an interruption by the Japanese in the Second World War. Australia continued to administrate both areas until the independence of the eastern half of the island – named Papua New Guinea – in 1975. The Dutch territories in the western half – known today as Irian Jaya or West Papua – came under the state of Indonesia when the Netherlands acknowledged its independence in 1949. The Solomon Islands became a British Protectorate in the 1890s and achieved independence in 1978, while the New Hebrides, now known as Vanuatu, was shared as an Anglo–French condominium before gaining independence in 1980.

In contrast, French Polynesia (which includes the Austral Islands, the Marquesas Islands and the Society Islands) and

Preceding pages: Miss Samoa Parade at the Teuila Festival, Apia, Samoa, 2003. Pageants, parades and performances are part and parcel of Independence Day celebrations throughout the Pacific. It was only in the second half of the twentieth century that colonial powers were relinquished and new independent states emerged across the Pacific. This image makes an interesting connection between Samoan traditional culture and European influence: the crowned model resembles the English female warrior Boadicea who fought against the Romans, while the floral arch frames this striking scene in Samoan fashion.

Opposite: Miss Samoa Parade, Teuila Festival, Apia, Samoa, 2003. The performance involves the unfolding of the dress, revealing the word 'Samoa' to the audience in ways that are reminiscent of the unfolding of barkcloth during life-cycle events marking marriage or death. These highly popular pageants – which people from all over the Pacific tune into on television – make powerful statements about the importance of the past in fabricating emerging identities in newly formed Pacific Island nations.

Right: Dancers from Lavengamalie College performing at the 85th birthday of King Tupou IV, Nuku'alofa, Tonga, 2003. National costumes comprising an assemblage of new materials such as plastic and cloth arranged in old designs are a hallmark of Pacific Independence Day celebrations. The costumes shown in the photograph are made mainly from leaves, with some plastic, and only last the day.

47

New Caledonia became French colonies in the 1840s and 1853 respectively, and remain so today. New Caledonia served as a penal colony until the early 1900s. In the mid-1990s, Mururoa, in French Polynesia, staged French nuclear tests that led to widespread protests across the globe.

The Hawaiian Islands were annexed by the United States in 1898 and became the fiftieth state of America in 1959. Guam and American Samoa remain territories of the US, while the Caroline Islands (which includes Pohnpei and Yap) formed the Federated States of Micronesia, though they retain strong political and economic links with the US, as does Palau (Belau), which gained independence from American administration in 1994.

Colonial rule paved the way for the economic exploitation of the Pacific Islands, and the advent of plantations and wage labour presaged the transformation of the Pacific landscape. Large parts of islands such as New Ireland and New Britain were turned over to the production of cash crops such as copra and oil palm. This led to the emergence of a shifting labour force, with ensuing economic migrations across the Pacific sometimes taking the form of enforced labour (known as blackbirding). Logging

operations, mining companies and, more recently, coffee manufacturers now stake claims to the wide range of natural resources available.

Many of the concerns of islanders about the environmental impact of these industries and experiences of the colonial past are captured in contemporary artworks and performances now practised by Pacific artists. Annual celebrations marking national independence days or the first arrival of the mission provide the backdrop for theatrical performances and colourful processions in which people act out aspects of the colonial past in chosen themes.

Economic opportunities and contingencies led many Pacific Islanders to move to the main centres of commerce in Australia, New Zealand and North America. In cities such as Auckland and Los Angeles, women selling handicrafts at local markets have played an important role in revitalizing Pacific diaspora communities. The effect of their wares is not merely economic: social issues are increasingly being voiced through fibre and cloth-based media, and woven net bags and printed T-shirts bear social and political slogans. These market places are now reinstating pride in the immigrant communities.

# 2

# TRADITIONAL
# PATTERN:
# TECHNIQUES
# AND MEDIA

Thread-based techniques of knotting, plaiting and looping were predominant in both the everyday and ceremonial uses of fibre arts across the Pacific. Before Europeans changed islanders' ways of living, almost every woman spent a good part of her day working with fibres, plaiting floor coverings, food wrappers, cooking containers, storage and carrying baskets, as well as special baskets for ceremonial events. Baskets came in different shapes and sizes depending on their original purpose, and there were distinct receptacles for a whole host of specific foodstuffs and other items. Common designs included baskets for collecting shellfish or crabs, storage for dried, cooked or freshly caught fish and other food, food platters and containers for clothes. Plaiting techniques were also used to make an array of different mats, which were designed as floor coverings, bedding or clothing (to wear as a wrap). Garments were made from the bark of the paper mulberry tree (barkcloth) or from finely rolled flax fibres. The dying, decorating and perfuming of all these coverings were as important as the processes of production that left their imprint in the texture of the design.

A survey of fibre-based techniques across the Pacific supports the existence of at least two contrasting types of media: string-based (cordage) and lattice-based (basketry). The basic distinction between cordage and basketry lies in the use of fibres of either unlimited (string) or limited (lattice) length in the product. Barkcloth, a felt-like material in which fibres are matted together, ambiguously falls inbetween these categories, and some even argue that it forms a distinct category altogether.

There are various definitions of cordage and basketry, although in this book we will follow the definitions outlined in Willemina Wendrich's *Who is Afraid of Basketry: A Guide to Recording Basketry and Cordage for Archaeologists and Ethnographers* (1991). In this illuminating manual, Wendrich defines basketry as, 'products in which raw (but not necessarily "natural") materials of limited length and shape are incorporated'. The term is thus used in *Pacific Pattern* to define any construction made out of lattice work, using fibres of limited length or with a shape that is specific to the raw material. It encompasses a class of artefacts that includes baskets, bags and mats. As a lattice-based medium, basketry brings the idea of containment to the fore – not only does the raw material retain its specific shape, but the production of basketry requires repetitive actions routinized in the human body. It requires physical skills of twisting the fibrous strands – of, say, coconut leaves or pandanus – to become a component of the product.

Cordage is defined by Wendrich as a class of fibre-based artefacts in which the fibres have been worked into uniform cylindrical strands of unlimited length, as well as artefacts obtained by knotting such strands. One of Wendrich's most important observations is her view of cordage as any construction made out of string that is formed according to a plan visualized on the basis of geometric principles alone. Cordage thus externalizes an idea that outlasts the medium. This is in sharp contrast to basketry in which it is not the externalized idea that is thought to last, but a form deriving from the raw material itself. In contrast to Wendrich, who places cordage midway on a continuum that stretches from basketry to textiles, the main differentiation in the Pacific is between basketry and cordage, with products such as barkcloth, quilts and imported fabric occupying the space inbetween.

The techniques within these categories will be outlined here. Today, many incorporate innovative forms and new materials.

Preceding pages, left: Diana Leaupepe weaving a fine mat, Teuila Festival, Apia, Samoa, 2003. Right: New Guinean woman carrying child in a string bag, *c.* 1900. The looping technique used to make string bags allows the container to expand and contract.

Right: Quickly made, disposable coconut palm frond baskets, Port Vila market, Vanuatu, 2004.

Opposite, above, left: Vaineiti Ngariu weaves a coconut palm frond basket, Mangaia, Cook Islands, 2003.

Opposite, above, right: Mata Lyon splits coconut fronds, Rarotonga, Cook Islands, 2003.

Opposite, below: Woman preparing pandanus leaves, Rakahanga Atoll, Cook Islands, 1991.

Preceding pages, clockwise from top left: Karerua Torotoro using a cowrie shell on pandanus leaves, Mangaia, Cook Islands, 2003; large mat made from coconut palm fronds, Rakahanga Atoll, Cook Islands, 1991; drying pandanus leaves spread out on the grass, Popua village, Nuku'alofa, Tonga, 2003.

Left: A group of women wearing matching dresses and weaving fine mats from pandanus leaves, Siumu Sasde, Upolu, Samoa, 2003. Removable walls of coconut frond mats provide shade and ventilation.

Below: Shirley Kalchichi makes sinnet, Pango village, Efate, Vanuatu, 2004. Sinnet is plaited or rolled fibre used to make lengths of cordage. The fibre can be taken from the hibiscus stem, the husk of the green or mature coconut, or from nettle plants. As preparation for the twining of the fibre, the fibres are soaked in lagoon waters, peeled, beaten, dried and finally rolled in a process that takes several weeks.

Opposite: Shirley Kalchichi creates sinnet, Pango village, Efate, Vanuatu, 2003. Sitting on a pandanus mat, she is employing a method of 'finger twisting' to make a long two-ply strand of cordage. Finger twisting requires the use of a long strand of fibres. This strand is doubled over, and the looped end held in the left hand. The left hand maintains a tension, while the right fingers and thumb tightly twist the top strand away from the body. As the top strand is twisted, it is brought down to cross in front of the lower strand. The crossed area is held in the left hand, and the strand now in the upper position (formerly in the lower position) is twisted and crossed in front of the lower strand. This process is continued to make a long two-ply strand of cordage.

What will become apparent is the sequential, highly ordered and rhythmic quality of work involved with fibre.

## String-based Media

Cordage used to bind, lash, tie, weave and sew is commonly referred to by terms such as thread, string, twine and rope. Activities dependent on cordage include fishing with a line or a net, using a bow and arrow, and the manufacture of clothing.

Historically, cordage has been made from a variety of different plant and animal fibres, but these days synthetic alternatives are also used. Although contemporary cordage is usually machine-manufactured and bought in stores, traditional fibre cordage – twisted and spun by hand – has remained an economical and widely used medium throughout the Pacific.

String-based media are made through a variety of techniques of which twining is the most common in the Pacific. Twining involves the twisting of two or more fibres by rolling

Left: Detail of woven armour outfit, Kiribati, Micronesia. The diamond-shaped motifs are worked in black human hair.

them on the thigh or between the fingers into a single strand called sinnet.

In Kapingamarangi, an island to the south of the Truk in Micronesia, cordage of local manufacture was still in constant use in the 1940s, when the New Zealand curator Sir Peter Buck conducted his ground-breaking research there. Locally grown fibres were obtained from coconut husk (*puru*), the inner bark of the wild hibiscus (*hau*), breadfruit (*kuru*) and *warenga*, a member of the nettle family. Strips of hibiscus bast were used for ordinary tying, while pandanus and green coconut leaves were used to bind food packages. The most prominent fibre used for cordage, however, was made from the husk of the green drinking coconut. (In Polynesia, in contrast, the mature husk is still preferred.)

Sir Peter Buck offers us a detailed description of the manufacture of this cordage, paraphrased here to underscore the highly ordered nature of the work, which demands precise hand movements according to a pre-planned geometric design. As preparation for the twining of the fibre, the husk segments are soaked in the lagoon waters for about a month. Usually, a shallow

Left: Man in woven armour suit constructed from thick-netted coconut fibres, Kiribati, Micronesia, *c.* 1900. The suit is made from several parts including the helmet, shoulder and arm pieces as well as body and leg suit. The sword is coconut fibre cord stiffened with wooden strips and edged with sharks' teeth.

Opposite, left: A Samoan chief, with a fly whisk made of sinnet cordage, at the 7th Festival of Pacific Arts, Apia, Samoa, 1996.

Opposite, right: Detail of coconut husk dried for the preparation of sinnet, Pango village, Efate, Vanuatu, 2004.

hole is scooped out under knee-deep water, husk segments laid in it, and then some sand scooped over the top. Large coral stones are laid on top to mark the spot and to prevent the segments from drifting away. When required, the husks are removed. The short inner fibres are torn off and the outer skin peeled off, and then the husks are washed in the water. The husk is beaten until it becomes pale yellow and silky in appearance. (When mature husk is used, as in Samoa, the removed inter-fibrous material, gathered next to the pile of stones on which the husk is beaten, emits a bad odour.) The beaten bunches are then dried in the sun before being rolled into single strands of string.

The preliminary step to making cordage is the separation of the required amount of fibre from the bunch of beaten husks, before rolling it into individual strands. To do this, a woman sits cross-legged on the floor, as the fibres are rolled on her bare thigh. She picks a bunch of fibres with her left hand and proceeds with the forefinger and thumb of her right hand to detach the quantity of fibres necessary to form the required strands for the cord. This depends on the intended thickness of the sinnet, which in turn is determined by the purpose of the cord. Short pieces are then removed from the strand until it is of even thickness, with the ends thinning off slightly as a matter of practicality in case further strands need to be added to lengthen the cord.

The twining of cord in Micronesia is two-ply compared to the three-ply cord produced all over Polynesia. In Micronesia, a general distinction is made between a right-hand cord, associated with the land, and a left-hand cord, associated with the sea. The left-handed technique is used to produce a coarser cord with thicker strands but a looser twist. These cords stretch more easily and are used to lash houses and canoes.

## Artefacts of Cordage: Cloaks, Capes and Helmets

Museum collections tell us about a variety of artefacts that were made from cordage. In the republic of Kiribati (formerly known as the Gilbert Islands), and reportedly further west in the Caroline Islands as well, a unique form of woven coconut fibre body-armour was worn as a protection against a deadly weapon

studded with sharks' teeth that was used in fighting. Certain objects made of wood, shell, feathers and cordage signified varying degrees of rank. In Samoa, for example, a baton-like handle with sinnet cord at one end was known as a fly whisk and denoted chiefly status. In the Caroline Islands and in some parts of the Solomon Islands, loom weaving continues to be practised, as does the making of beautiful sashes and currency cloths from banana fibre. The construction of fishing nets and traps represents the most widespread usage of cordage, though it is not limited to functional use. Across the non-Austronesian region of language groups of New Guinea, looped net bags (*bilums*) are used as 'carriers' instead of baskets, and they are also a quintessential part of everyday wear.

The string bag, or *bilum* as it is known in Papua New Guinea, has become an emblem of national identity. Made from both natural or synthetic cordage, it is produced extensively across the Highlands region using a looping technique. This enables the fibrous openwork form to expand and contract in size, depending on the load inside, leading many to remark on its womb-like character. String bags are made in various sizes using dyed cordage to create differing patterns.

Above: String bag made from vegetable fibre with feather decoration, Telefomin, Papua New Guinea.

Overleaf, clockwise from top left: Te Aue Davis weaves a Maori feather cloak, Mangere, New Zealand, 2004. Cloaks decorated fully with feathers seem to have appeared in the mid-nineteenth century, becoming popular by the end of the century, and remain prestigious garments today. Feather cloaks are often extremely colourful, using pheasant, parrot, peacock and domestic fowl plumage.

A detail of peacock and albatross feathers decorating a basket made of flax. The maker is Te Aue Davis of Mangere, New Zealand, 2004.

As gifts to relatives and close friends, it is often said that a woman makes a string bag in the image of the recipient. Although string bags are mainly produced and used by women to store and carry garden produce as well as young infants, their use also extends to the world of men who utilize special string bags covered with feathers to contain secret paraphernalia.

Some of the most famous artefacts in museum collections using net-based construction are the feather capes and cloaks of the Maori-speaking peoples in Hawaii, Tahiti and New Zealand. These are beautiful products of knotted cordage in which the craftsmen displayed a high standard of technical skill. The explorer Captain James Cook writes of a feather cloak and helmet, which he considered elegant, 'The surface might be compared to the thickest and richest velvet, which they resemble, both as to the feel and the glossy appearance.' Capes and cloaks became a monopoly of the higher chiefs and marked their social distinction and rank. They became regalia, instead of normal apparel, and were prohibited to commoners and women. To mark their gendered nature further, the garments were made entirely by men.

Different techniques of construction existed, all using cordage to attach the feathers, and it is again Sir Peter Buck who has provided us with the most detailed descriptions. In New Zealand, the feather cloaks were made of flax fibre, and continue to be so, using a form of finger weaving in which the feathers are attached to the warps by the turns of an interlocking weft. In Tahiti, the feather cloak that formed part of a mourner's costume was made by attaching bunches of large feathers to a long cord by means of overhand knots (this type of knot can be used at the end of a string, either to prevent it from unravelling or to thicken the end of a string to prevent another knot from loosening, and when the same knot is used in the middle of a string to bind it is called a half knot). A thinner cord tied to the feather bunches helped to maintain the inter-bunch spacing.

The Hawaiian technique consisted of tying bunches of small feathers to a netting foundation. The main feature of this procedure was the preparation of the netting, knotted to the required size, and the attachment of the feathers in small bunches to the net mesh with a separate binding thread. The feathers were obtained from a variety of birds: small feathers from forest birds and large feathers from domesticated fowl and various seabirds.

Helmets are another example of traditional Hawaiian fibre arts. They were made in different styles to reflect the social position of the wearer. The crested helmets covered with coloured feathers were part of the regalia of high chiefs and kings and thus complemented the feather cloaks. Other helmets were decorated with human hair or mushroom-like ornaments, and were worn by warriors and lesser chiefs. Instead of netting, the helmet had as its foundation a cap made of the split aerial rootlets of the *ie'ie* (*Freycinetia arborea*), as were other parts of the helmet's foundation. The split rootlets are arranged in warps and wefts, and bound together in a form of finger weaving very like the technique used in weaving Maori cloaks.

## The Sacred Thread in Polynesia

The idea of the 'sacred' nature of the thread – which, according to Polynesian belief, possesses *mauri*, the spiritual essence that is thought to be contained in all living things and natural objects – is perhaps best described with the example of *ahu tapu*, or traditional Maori weaving. The weaving of garments made from flax fibre has undergone a remarkable revival in contemporary Maori society. While its techniques perpetuate ancient skills of traditional Maori weaving, as the fibres and dyes are those used by the ancestors, innovations in style and design are thriving.

By far the most widely used fibre for Maori clothing is obtained from what is commonly called New Zealand flax or flax-lily (*Phormium tenax*). Early European explorers compared the silkiness of its fibre to that of linen flax and applied the name, even though the New Zealand flax is unrelated to the flax family

of plants. It is highly versatile – long strips of leaf with good colour were used for plaited floor mats (*whariki*), shorter but strong and flexible leaves for baskets (*kete*), and long and strong fibres for the manufacture of fish nets. Early European visitors were excited by the fibre. In it, they saw possibilities for commercial rope-making, and perhaps textile manufacture. It soon became a lucrative trade item, of particular importance to the Maori in obtaining firearms, and whole communities became involved in the work of separating and preparing the fibre.

Regardless of the type of fibre or technique used, Maori weaving worked horizontally, from left to right. The work was traditionally kept upright with weaving sticks, but nowadays weavers sit on a chair, and the work is supported by a frame that stands on the floor. Today, as before, no weaving tools are used: the fingers simply manipulate the wefts. While the fibre is being woven, respect is shown for the material, which is believed to possess the spiritual essence, *mauri*.

The Maori belief in the sacred nature of thread indicates a profound significance attributed to string-based media that went beyond their overt function of binding. Associated with institutional forms of rank, such artefacts connote the prestige that is gained from possessing the means of linking conceptually different levels of existence, whether the dead and the living, or chiefly aristocrats and commoners.

# Lattice-based Media

Plaiting is a fibre-based technique used across the whole of the Pacific that involves the interlacing of three or more sets of elements in order to form a continuous surface.

Left: Detail of Te Aue Davis's weaving loom with a feather cloak, Mangere, New Zealand, 2004.

Right: Ake Master weaves coconut palm frond *rito* string, Rarotonga, Cook Islands, 2003. Delicate but strong, *rito* is the most valued material of many Pacific islands and comes from the unopened shoots at the top of the coconut palm.

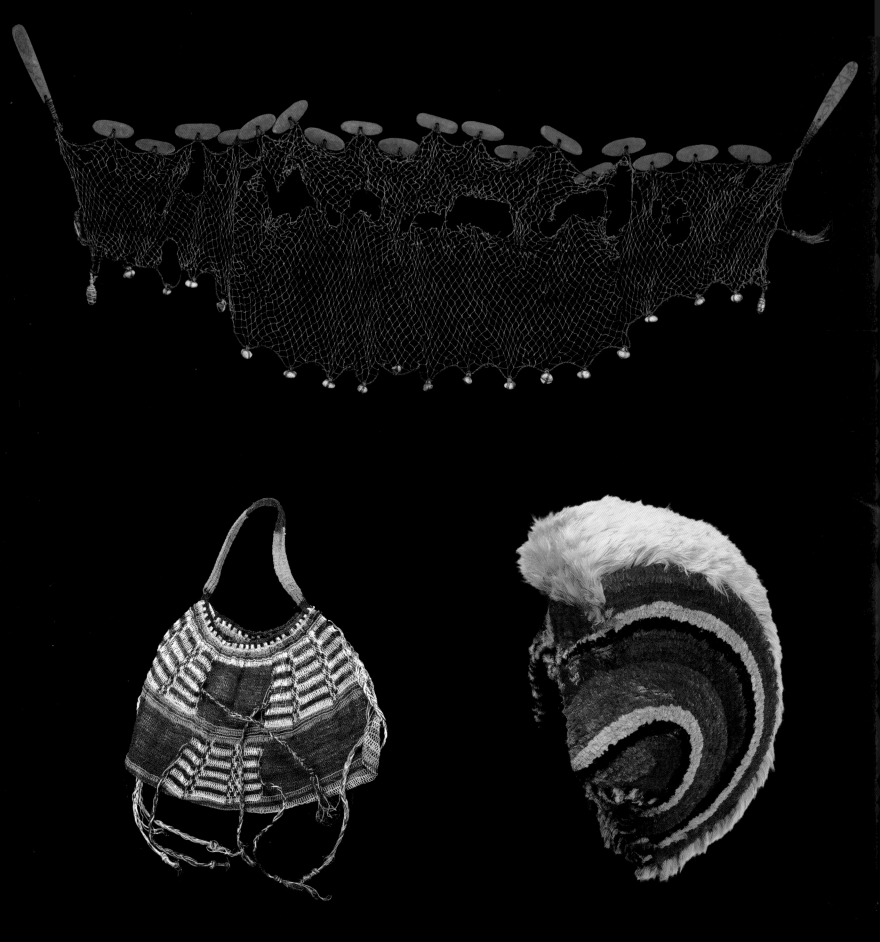

Opposite, above: Long rectangular vegetable fibre fishing net with twenty stone sinkers, two end ones encased in cane plaiting and eighteen wooden floats, New Britain, Papua New Guinea.

Opposite, below left: String bag made from acrylic fibre in geometric patterns of red, green, black and white on one side and green and white stripes on the other, Sepik River, Papua New Guinea.

Opposite, below right: Hawaiian crested helmets covered with coloured feathers were part of the regalia of high chiefs and kings and complemented the feather cloaks. At its foundation, the helmet had a cap made of the split aerial rootlets, which were arranged in warps and wefts and bound together in a form of finger weaving very like the technique used in weaving Maori cloaks.

Right: Tahitian dancer wearing a feather helmet at the 7th Festival of Pacific Arts, Apia, Samoa, 1996.

Compared to weaving, the technique of plaiting is relatively simple as the materials involved are usually stiffer and wider. Finger movements more easily accomplish the plaiting technical process, while those using cumbersome weaving technologies have sought mechanical assistance. Articles produced by plaiting include mats, baskets and wall dividers.

Plaiting designs follow a technique found across the Pacific, in which the wefts run at angles to the edges. Leaves of the coconut and pandanus palms provide the raw material, both of which appear in abundance across the Pacific. In general,

pandanus leaves have a higher social value than those of the coconut palm, as they are used for mats of a higher grade.

Although lowlier than the pandanus, the coconut palm is a valuable resource across the Pacific Islands, as the leaves provide a natural resource from which to make crude baskets very quickly without any preliminary treatment of the material. The coconut palm is an ideal plaiting medium for a number of important reasons. The key elements are the strong midrib and its protruding fronds. Palm fronds are characteristically parallel to each other, which means that alternate fronds can be easily

bent in opposite directions to provide the crossing wefts necessary for plaiting a check pattern. Thus, the palm fronds form ready-made wefts and their natural attachment to the leaf midrib does away with the necessity of fixing wefts at the starting edge. The palm leaf midrib is particularly versatile, and when it is split along its centre there is just enough thickness to support the fronds required. Women therefore lay the midrib closest to them for plaiting, using it as a base line during basket-making.

The simplest basket, created across the Pacific, is the *poroporo* – a Polynesian term referring to a flat platter with

Opposite, left: Pandanus basket, Apia, Samoa, 2003.

Opposite, right: Maori flax basket, known as *kete*, woven by Tui Romain, Auckland, New Zealand, 2004. *Kete* are made from strips of New Zealand flax. *Kete*-making is currently flourishing and the possession of such a basket is considered a badge of cultural identity.

Basket makers are appreciated for their skill and knowledge, and owners may take particular care of a basket out of respect for the artist.

Above, left: Pandanus basket, Apia, Samoa, 2003.

Above, right: Maori flax basket, *kete*, woven by Tui Romain, Auckland, New Zealand, 2004.

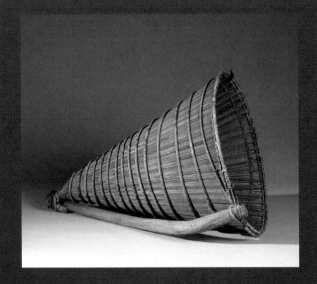

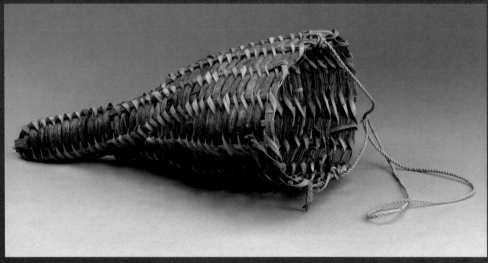

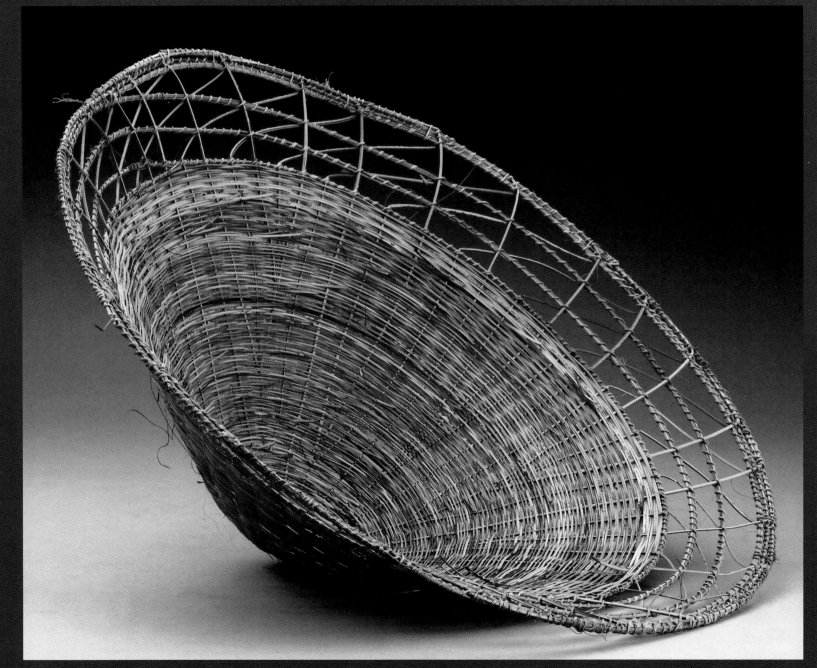

a check design. The platter is made from the left side of the coconut palm leaf midrib, separated from the right side and cut to size. With the midrib strip forming the leading edge and the shiny surface of the leaves facing upwards, women start plaiting from the left-hand side and work across towards the right. Counting off two fronds, the woman bends the third leaf back, towards the left, crossing over the second frond but passing underneath the first one. From this point on, however, she deals with the fronds in pairs, so that alternate fronds are bent back

Opposite, above left: Nineteenth-century fishing basket made from wickerwood, Samoa.

Opposite, above right: Fish trap from the Solomon Islands.

Opposite, below: Fish basket, shallow with pointed base, made from vegetable fibre and used for collecting

fish, Sepik River, Papua New Guinea.

Below: Maile Havila Tongai weaving a fibre placemat, Nuku'alofa market, Tonga, 2004.

## TECHNIQUES OF MAT-MAKING

Pandanus (or fine) mats are known as 'women's wealth' and are an important item of exchange in places such as Samoa, Vanuatu, the Cook Islands, Tahiti and Tonga. Such mats, which can take months if not years to complete, are extremely valuable. The following example takes you through the production of Samoan fine mats in particular, stage by stage.

1  First, the serrated edges of the pandanus leaves are removed and the spines on the back of the midrib trimmed off. Then a short incision to the dull underneath of the leaf is made, about 4 cm from the stub end. The underside of the leaf is carefully pulled away from the stub to the incision, so that the thin upper shiny leaf layer remains intact. After leaving the prepared leaves in the sun, they are then folded into 60 cm lengths and tied together into a bundle.

2  Heating the leaf bundle is the next important stage. This is done by placing the bundle – wrapped in a layer of protective green leaves – into a stone oven for about half an hour. Once removed, the leaves are straightened before the shiny upper layer of the leaf is carefully peeled away. The heating enables the easy separation of the upper from lower leaf.

3  The tips of three of the dull undersides of the leaves (the rest of which have been discarded) are knotted together, before the woman begins plaiting them together to make a single braid. She does this by placing the knot between her toes and stretching the plaits taut. The braid is used to secure other treated pandanus leaves, which the woman attaches as she moves up the length of the braid.

4  The leaves are submerged in the sea and soaked for around two weeks, after which they appear bleached. They are then cut free from the braid and left out in the sun to dry. Each leaf frond is split lengthwise down the midrib, and each half is wound around the fingers into rolls.

5  The weft plaits for the fine mats face even more preparation before the actual plaiting can begin. The underneath of each of the pandanus fronds is carefully rubbed down with a shell scraper, on a scraping board, removing excess fibrous material. The leaves are then split along their length, from a little before the end to the tip. The unsplit end thus holds together a number of split wefts.

Opposite, from top (1) to bottom (4):
(1): The weaving of fine mats in Upolu, Samoa, 2003. Pandanus mat-making is something of an art in Samoa. Fine mats are characterized by thin narrow wefts in the check, and by decoration with fringes and red feathers. Women have exclusive control of the production and distribution of the mats, which are highly prestigious and presented as gifts during life-cycle events such as births, deaths and marriages.
(2): Detail of pandanus mat with feather fringe, Pango, Efate, Vanuatu, 2004.
(3): Manu Jimmy weaves a pandanus mat, Pango village, Efate, Vanuatu, 2004.
(4): Tui Romain weaves a New Zealand flax *kete* basket, Auckland, New Zealand, 2004.

Right: Leikave Kalserei weaves a pandanus mat, Takare, Efate, Vanuatu, 2004. Fibre patterns in mats and baskets are created using dyed pandanus strips as well as natural ones, reversed to give a contrasting effect.

Overleaf, left, clockwise from top left: Fine mat detail, Siumu Sasde, Upolu, Samoa, 2003; detail of a pandanus mat, Apia, Samoa, 2004; detail of a Niuean pandanus mat, Auckland, New Zealand, 2004; detail of a pandanus mat, Rarotonga, Cook Islands, 2003; detail of a pandanus basket by Chantal Bule Tare, Port Vila, Vanuatu, 2004; detail of a pandanus basket by Chantal Bule Tare, Port Vila, Vanuatu, 2004.

Overleaf, right: Tele Alo weaves a pandanus basket, Laulii, Samoa, 2003.

towards the left-hand side to produce a check pattern. The same basic technique is used to plait other coconut frond artefacts such as sleeping mats, food containers, bags and hats.

Although the coconut palm leaf appears to constrain variations in pattern and form, Pacific women are particularly adept at creating a multitude of designs by employing various plaiting techniques. In New Ireland, Papua New Guinea, for example, coconut baskets are quintessential to differentiating village identities: simply by noticing a basket and the way it is

carried, one can infer the village in which the basket's owner resides. Baskets may be carried on the shoulder, the head or in the hand, as well as hung on the end of a stick that is balanced over the shoulder. In each case, a basket's form is ideally suited to the way it is carried, with larger ones worn on the shoulder or on the head for support. Medium-sized ones, meanwhile, are suspended over the back attached with long straps that wrap across the forehead, while some small ones, carried in the hand, are used for keeping personal items such as betel nut, tobacco and money.

The *rito* hat – made by weaving together the unopened shoots at the top of the coconut palm – is a distinguishing feature of contemporary Cook Island attire. *Rito* and pandanus hats are worn to church as part of one's 'Sunday best'. There is seemingly no limit to the design, decoration and patterns produced in soft fibre. Clockwise from top left: *Rito* hat, Rarotonga, Cook Islands, 2003;

*rito* hat, Cook Island Christian Church in Arorangi, Rarotonga, Cook Islands, 2003; pandanus hat, Rarotonga, Cook Islands, 2003; *rito* hat, Auckland, New Zealand, 2004; *rito* hat, Otara, Auckland, New Zealand, 2004; *rito* hat, Auckland, New Zealand, 2004; Niuean Pandanus hat, Auckland, New Zealand, 2004; *rito* hat, Cook Island Christian Church, Manihiki, Cook Islands, 1991.

Like the string bag, baskets are an essential component of everyday wear and remain almost inconspicuous. On important occasions, however, such as Sunday church gatherings in the Cook Islands, specially woven hats are donned by women. These hats, often decorated with coloured bands of shells and adorned with floral motifs, are consciously fashioned to the wearer's dress, drawing attention to her prestigious attire. While these examples illustrate the robustness and versatility of the coconut palm leaf, the source of prestige and quality in fibre arts are dominated by the leaf of the pandanus. Often pandanus is

preferred because its fine weave and silk-like qualities simulate the texture of skin.

Pandanus leaves can be used to make a large variety of articles. In its diverse use of pandanus, Kiribati is typical of any place in the Pacific: for example, objects made from pandanus leaf include roof sheets (*kaurama rouhara*), sails (*ra*), baskets (*kata*), fishermen's hats (*kopai*) and, of course, mats (*kahara*). There, as in other key mat-making areas such as Tonga and Samoa, there are five different types of mat: *kahara moenga*, ordinary sleeping mats, a more elaborate sleeping mat known

as *wawa*, coarse mats used for covering the floor (*kahara te*), smaller mats used as skirts by women in taro (a root vegetable) plantations (*kahara turi*) and fine mats traditionally worn by men (*kahara tangata*).

In Samoa, pandanus mat-making is something of an art, which is reflected in the diversity of their use and manufacture. Whereas crude coconut-palm leaf mats were made before European exploration to cover carved wooden figures during religious ceremonies, pandanus mats are commonplace today. There are sleeping mats, others to cover the floor or separate one

Left: Knotted spirit house made from sinnet, Fiji, nineteenth century. These miniature spirit houses were kept in temples and served as a container for particular spirits.

Right: Trap for moray eel, made of shoots and slim branches of salt bush, bound with coconut fibre cord, Kiribati, Micronesia.

room from the next, and fine mats that could be wrapped around the body as a form of clothing. Like other fibre arts of the Pacific, mat-making remains firmly in the women's realm.

Fine mats – the most valued of all mats – are characterized by thin narrow wefts in the check and decorations of fringes and red feathers. Women have exclusive control of the production and distribution of these highly prestigious mats, which are given as gifts during life-cycle events such as births, deaths and marriages. To receive a fine mat as a gift is a great honour; moreover, gifting of fine mats both affirms and increases the status of the donor. Fine mats are also worn during important public events, where they take on a much broader contextual significance, such as indicating the wearer's status and relationship to the event.

Making Samoan fine mats involves months, even years, of work and entails several stages of preparation (see page 72 for a complete step-by-step explanation). Women employ a series of technical processes in the plaiting of fine mats. One can only imagine the intense labour involved in the plaiting process. The principal task is to double the weft plaits, thus allowing the dull leaf surfaces to be placed back-to-back and the shiny surfaces to face outwards on both sides. A three-ply braid – that is, three leaf fronds interlaced with one another to form a tightly bound braid – is used to secure the leaf edges. On average, these mats contain around twelve pandanus leaf fronds per inch, but some of the more valuable mats incorporate many more. To complete the mat, one or more borders of red parrot feathers are used, sewn on as rows parallel to the lower edge.

Today, the value of fine mats is largely associated with the size of the mat, which can range from 1 metre to as much as 3.6 metres. The smaller grades are now considered so commonplace that they are given away in bundles of five or six at a time at

important events in the life of the household, marking weddings, birthdays and funerals. The fine mats of today are made in a few weeks or less, with many of the old steps in manufacture omitted. This can be explained by the fact that coloration can now be added with the use of dyes or coloured threads rather than being wrought from the raw materials by inducing chemical changes from soaking, burying or burning. This is also the case for cordage, as buying nylon or cotton has come to replace the arduous preparation of plant fibre in order for it to be pliable and appropriately coloured.

## From Utility to Sanctity

In Micronesia, special traps were made for catching eels. These elaborately constructed devices resemble traditional houses, complete with pitched roof, doors and windows made from wood strips bound together with cordage. Eels have mythical status across the Pacific and are often depicted in stories that feature their transformation into a coconut palm. Like the coconut, the eel is characterized by its migratory habits, as both arrive along the shoreline of Pacific Islands during certain seasons of the year. Their arrival, which coincides with times of heightened ritual activity and spiritual presence, is thus construed to be a sign of their spiritual power. As eels are thereby associated with growth and bringers of life and light, the form of the trap is seemingly fitting: in a region of the world where spirits are attributed human-like qualities, it is not surprising to find that model houses are designed to trap eels and spirits alike.

Designs in cordage and basketry are thus far from merely utilitarian. In both, the fibre medium acts as a stable reference point for thinking about genealogical relations in interdependent ways. The limited transformation of basketry, which retains the shape of its raw materials and the traces of the bodily involvement in its construction, visually contains temporal movements and relations within the articulation of a spatial medium. In this way a mat can be seen as a lineage's lifeblood, rather than its representation, fixing persons to places at instances in time. Cordage, on the other hand, with its transformation of materials into ongoing, unlimited spans, is uniquely capable of linking together different orders of beings, the visible and the invisible, whose momentary entanglement facilitates a notion of a continuous temporal genealogy that is dependent on repeated ritual performances. It is this capacity of fibre arts to visualize complex ideas of time and space that lies at the heart of Pacific societies.

Mats and baskets are thus renowned for the value that is attached to them as heirlooms of a special kind. In Samoa, for example, women's production of fine mats plaited from pandanus fibre, and the use of these mats in significant exchanges marking the life cycle of a household, enable some of them to hold high-ranking titles and to maintain a political presence. Although the mats may, at first glance, look alike, there are special ones – usually old and richly decorated with feathers along the fringes – associated with important titles of rank that grant access to lineage land. These most treasured mats carry the title of their owner, and the efforts at preserving these often very fragile objects tell us a lot about the value attributed to them. Such mats are stored in treasure trunks and are only passed on to the next generation at the inauguration of a new titleholder. In contrast, other lesser-ranking mats are poured, in their thousands, into the important exchanges marking life and

death, and are given in bundles of five or ten at a time, in such great numbers that they are piled up to look like haystacks. Fine mats, on the other hand, are considered so important that at times a person may decide to hold his or her own funeral distributions while still alive in order to ensure that articles go to the correct recipients. In Samoa, fine mats still 'outrank' other goods, including money, and continue to add weight to the exchanges of other goods and services.

Across the Pacific, cordage was also assigned outstanding ritual significance that complemented the capabilities of mats and baskets to punctuate life-cycle events. In Hawaii, a sacred cord ('aha) traditionally acted as the reference point to genealogy: it was the braiding of the cord by the king that represented not just the king's relationship with the gods, but also the connecting force of genealogy that, 'binds together all other genealogies, since it is their reference point and the locus of their legitimacy and truth', as the anthropologist Valerio Valeri describes it in his classic *Kingship and Sacrifice: Ritual and Sacrifice in Ancient Hawaii* (1985). In contrast to Samoan fine mats, the cord of Hawaiian kingship was not inherited – the undoing of the king's sacred cord dissolved the social bond between the king, his subjects and the gods. The strands obtained from the undoing of the cords were woven into caskets in which the bones of the king were enshrined.

The Hawaiian sacred cord represented the king through association rather than resemblance, in a similar way to the representation of the gods. The cord was given processional value, as the processes of binding and undoing to which the cord was subjected constituted the mystical, corporate body of kingship. The binding of the cord has resonances across the Pacific. In ancient Tahiti, the binding of cordage also formed the most

Left: Pandanus mats as gifts for the bride's family, Mele, Efate, Vanuatu, 2004. Presentations form a vital part of life-cycle ceremonies on the islands.

important ritual act in *to'o*, a figure made of tightly knotted cordage whose unravelling took place at the height of rituals of succession. This figure was a composite object, generally made of a piece of hard wood with an elongated shape like a club or a stick, covered with layers of tightly bound cordage. Its height was indicative of the value ascribed to it. The correlation between a ranked polity of figures and social rank was given regular and formal expression in a ritual called *pa'iatua*, which means the 'gathering and undressing of the gods'. The stick remained completely invisible, covered in a tight binding of cordage called *'aha*. The binding was made of plaits of cords from the fibres of the coconut palm, which covered and interleaved layers of barkcloth, and the whole stick was decorated with feathers of different colours.

Another example of the importance afforded to cordage comes from ancient Fiji, where tightly bound cordage formed the basis for a scaled-down model of a spirit house (*bure kalou*). Miniature temples or shrines of this kind were kept in a large temple and served as the dwelling place for certain types of spirit, notably *luve ni wai*, which are small water spirits. Small figures made from whale ivory were often housed inside. These figures were traded from Tonga, where craftsmen excelled at working with the teeth of the sperm whale.

These examples point to the significance of cordage as a means of linking – through acts of binding and untying that can be repeated over and over again – the separate temporal and spatial domains of the world of the living and the world of the dead. Cordage is thus a crucial material metaphor across the Pacific, as it resurfaces at those key moments in society when ideas of renewal come to the fore.

Corporate clan unity, on the other hand, is manifest materially in the planar surface of containers plaited from plant fibre into lattice-work designs. The idea of diagonally interlocking plant fronds may even be foregrounded in the carving of planes in wood. That the shape and size of lattice-work depends on the constituent plant, whose precise figuration differs with every product, underscores the contingent nature of this medium, and serves as an outward sign of the historical connections that may be seen to prevail among people.

An example of the co-presence of cordage and lattice-work, and their corresponding ideas of continuous and discontinuous time, can be found in the funerary arts of northern New Ireland in Island Melanesia. Here, the infinite potential of string-based fibre on the one hand, and the finite and constrained shape limited to lattice-work fibre arts on the other, mediate a potentially devastating contradiction between a notion of identity that is traced along the mother's line, and a right to land that is transferred along the father's line.

The strength of the matrilineal clan in this society depends, to a large extent, on the production of fibre-based, woven structures, *warwara malangan*, whose circular configuration connotes their infinite, cyclical conception. These *warwara malangan* commemorate only the female dead (which includes those males who die prior to initiation and are thus assigned female status irrespective of their biological sex). At the same time as identity is transferring down the female line through these string-based artworks, ownership of land depends on the production of carved wooden sculptures that commemorate men whose lives were associated with the land. The wooden sculpture is a container for the spirit of the deceased person and reflects the history of a social group in a particular place. The idea of a container is reinforced through their visual allusions to basketry, made by incisions that create planes as if they were plaited fronds woven together: characteristic shapes and forms that are specific to the raw material and, by analogy, to the local groups.

The valuable lesson brought about through a concern with techniques forces us to confront the way in which ideas are carried by the materiality of things. While a history of Pacific design is certainly inseparable from a history of its societies, we must thus go beyond an explanation of its place in social contexts. As the architectural historian Adrian Forty has suggested in his book *Objects of Desire* (1986), 'design brings ideas and beliefs up against the material realities of production'. Design thus allows for the mental to commune with the

material and vice versa, and for complex ideas to take tangible forms, which themselves may elicit new ideas. Therefore, as Forty convincingly argues, design history is not a matter of changes in form being stages of a 'progressive evolution' that propels design in the direction of progress, but rather it casts into tangible forms ideas about who we are and how we should behave in a changing world. When we turn to the contemporary world of design in fibre and fabric that predominates across the Pacific, we shall see how useful this perspective will turn out to be.

Opposite, above left: Woven effigy, *to'o*, representing a minor deity, Society Islands, eighteenth century. The figure consists of a wooden interior around which is wrapped a length of knotted sinnet with red feathers placed inside.

Opposite, below right: Wooden malanggan male figure collected by Romilly from New Ireland, Papua New Guinea, in 1884. Above: Matautia Ieriko Niulevaea being dressed for title bestowal ceremony, Utufa'alalafa, Upolu, Samoa, 2003.

# CONTEMPORARY PATTERN: MATERIALITY AND MODERNITY

3

Since the first Europeans arrived in the eighteenth century, a huge and highly visible change in fibre arts has taken place in the Pacific. The importation of fabrics, their rapid uptake and, in some cases, their radical alteration raises issues critical to our understanding of the role of cordage and basketry in cultural change in the Pacific.

Fabric not only resembles barkcloth, but when it was transformed by shredding or unpicking and incorporated into nets, mats and baskets, it took on the strip or thread-like qualities associated with locally available plant fibres. It was this material link entertained by imported fabric with cordage, basketry and barkcloth that gave fabric the possibility to emulate the social and ritual significance already assumed by fibre.

The mass importation of fabrics and second-hand clothing into the Pacific did not result in the wholesale displacement of cordage, basketry and barkcloth, but led to the florescence of needlecraft technologies which resulted in novel forms of material expression throughout the Pacific. The Papua New Guinean *meri bilaus*, a type of 'Mother Hubbard' smock, the Hawaiian *holokû*, a free-flowing ankle-length dress, and the Niuean and Tahitian *tiputa*, a poncho-like barkcloth garment, all emerged as the result of needlecraft technologies.

Imported needlecraft technologies such as sewing, embroidery and crocheting, which are today practised throughout the Pacific, enabled the modification of traditional fibre arts using either locally available or imported materials or a combination of both. Patchwork quilts made from shredded fabric and hand-stitched with needle and coloured thread in the Cook Islands, for example, as well as the technology of sewing itself – embodied in the Singer sewing machine in places such as the Papuan Gulf – are considered essential wedding gifts today. It is unthinkable to get married or achieve social recognition without being given a Singer sewing machine or a patchwork quilt.

New fabric products reflected the transformations sweeping the Pacific in the latter half of the nineteenth century. A heightened concern with fibres from fabric thus ensued. Not only was this concern for the modification of fabric shared by Pacific Islanders alone, but it was also an overriding concern for the newcomers to the Pacific – the evangelical missionaries.

Clothing Pacific Islanders was paramount in the minds of the missionaries from the outset since they saw the adoption of clothing as an outward sign of conversion to Christianity, as they impressed on converts Christian values associated with managing time, place and body. On sighting clothed New Irelanders, the Methodist missionary George Brown recorded with relative optimism, 'I was glad to see Le Bera (the chief) clothed in a shirt and waistcloth, and his wives and daughters each wearing a handkerchief or small piece of cloth.' Indeed, the ready adoption of clothing on the part of Pacific Islanders heightened the resolve of Christian missionaries, many of whom had struggled to maintain a foothold in often remote and untamed frontiers where they were faced with constant threats of hostility, intimidation and violence.

With their belief that clothing brought with it a new moral economy of the body and mind, the missionaries correctly recognized the potential power of clothing. However, they failed to grasp the true significance of clothing in the Pacific. For Pacific Islanders, its importance lay in preconceptions – the attribution of life-giving qualities to fibre and fabric, which they viewed as vehicles of spiritual power.

## The Importance of Cloth

Pacific Islanders' fervent desire for cloth and clothing was inspired by its material qualities, particularly its 'whiteness' and 'luminosity', which demanded immediate action – cutting, sewing and folding – to harness and control the power contained within its folds. Many sources testify to the importance attributed to light in Polynesian ritual in particular, which derives from a conception of the world as having a dual composition: an exterior, wild and nocturnal world, which was the source of light and life;

Preceding pages: Plastic leis on display in the market of Port Vila, Efate, Vanuatu, 2004. Flower garlands are worn on all important occasions on the head or around the neck.

Opposite: Edna Manemut sews shirts, Port Vila market, Efate, Vanuatu, 2004.

Overleaf, left: Tongan woman, with jewelry, ornate fibre and fabric dress and a fan, c. 1900.

Page 87, left: Susan Moses with women on sewing machines, Esprito Santos, Vanuatu, 1997.

Pages 87–89: Ediline Kaluatman sews a 'Mother Hubbard'-style dress, Pango village, Efate, Vanuatu, 2004.

and an interior, domestic and diurnal world that depended upon the harnessing of light and life from the invisible and immaterial (such as the world of the gods or ancestors).

Cloth-like fibre in Polynesia always played a profound role in the life-giving and life-affirming ceremonies associated with marriage and investiture; yet this was only after brownish bark or darkened plant fronds were arduously lightened and given luminous yellow and reddish colouring through such laborious techniques as the washing, burying and staining of fibres. The patterning techniques of line and frond, with shiny additions such as shells and feathers, served to contain and domesticate light. The exploitation of light's reflective qualities turned pattern into an effective mediator with the immaterial world, whose life-giving qualities were further enhanced through the perfuming of fibrous pattern.

White, ready patterned and coloured (and sometimes even odorous) stitched cloth offered new technical possibilities for harnessing luminosity. By sheer coincidence, the fabric which Europeans had brought to barter, together with glass beads and mirrors, was often of a vivid red or blue as they thought that they could attract people by the colour and dazzle of their wares. As the material embodiment of light, clothing required harnessing, yet the manner in which it was domesticated differed substantially across the Pacific. We can see from historical archives and museum collections how, in some parts of the Pacific, patterned clothing was selectively appropriated to be worn on the body, or was worn with an additional layer of plant-fibre cloth; while in other parts, plain-coloured cloth was ripped into shreds before being woven into new composite patterns that often incorporated a multiplicity of clashing and vibrant colours. In New Georgia (the Solomon Islands), much clothing was stored in houses, rather than

worn – hidden away from sight – only to be revealed for exchanges during ritual ceremonies. In fact, the innovative use of stitched cloth across the Pacific tells a story of material translation, involving the transposition of cordage and basketry techniques, and of the material qualities of the line and the frond, into sewing and patching and the surface qualities of the stitch and the hem.

## Sewing and the Body Politic

The nineteenth-century missionaries who arrived in the Pacific with cloth and clothing as weapons of conversion also carried ideals of appropriate gender behaviour from Europe and North America, where the Industrial Revolution had seen a radical shift in notions of family and femininity that had reinforced the ideal of the woman's rightful place being in the home. Convinced of physical and moral differences between men and women, missionaries regarded women as the weaker sex and deplored their participation in activities outside the household. This attitude came to be reflected in the style of dress the missionaries imposed on Pacific women. While the clothes for men permitted physical labour, those manufactured for the Pacific women were tailored to restrict them to sitting quietly at home sewing, rather than working in the gardens, carrying firewood or harvesting shellfish on the reef.

In a move of profound consequence, Anglican missionaries introduced skirts and blouses, known today as *meri bilaus*, according to nineteenth-century ideals, across Papua New Guinea and Island Melanesia. Presbyterian missionaries created a similar style of dress for the Pacific market that was long and loose, and had elbow-length sleeves. These were often called 'Mother Hubbards', a designation that marked them as specifically 'native'.

Although these dresses were European in character, their introduction to the Pacific signalled a distinction between expatriate and indigenous that also paved the way for a vision of modernity that came to be distinctly 'Pacific'.

While the restrictive style of dresses may have derived from the missionaries' idealization of women's domestic role, the missions also managed to reinforce the association of women with the house through the introduction of technologies to produce and maintain clothing. Sewing techniques and the general care of clothing, including the washing and drying of clothes, became inseparably linked to the conversion of women, who were already responsible for the production of indigenous clothing. Sewing, and the tasks surrounding dressing, had consequences both for the conduct of spiritual life in Pacific communities and for the perception of gender roles. While in island cultures such as Vanuatu the production of plaited pandanus textiles or grass-skirts was linked to the seasonal agricultural cycle, the introduction of sewing dislocated women from these cycles and turned the care for clothing into a daily, unceasing task.

However, clothing the Pacific was not as straightforward as either the missionaries or market expected. Plant-fibre clothing, such as grass-skirts, were long considered more practical as they could be washed in seawater. According to the anthropologist and curator Lissant Bolton, in southern Vanuatu women continued to wear plant-fibre skirts on weekdays until about 1970, and they still prefer them as convenient clothing for work in the garden, reserving clothes handed out from the mission for Sunday wear. In addition, cloth was not always in ready supply and did not always arrive in appropriate colours. Bolton reports that for Vanuatu the missionary perception of a local predilection for bright colours

conflicted with local views that limited the donning of colour as a privilege of status. She recalls that on the island of Ambrym inhabitants had to acquire the right to wear both red and yellow, a fact that severely constrained the choice of suitable dress-material until the 1960s, when ritual restrictions were finally lifted from clothing.

In Tonga, the preference expressed by missionaries that people should wear white clothing as a lesson in industriousness, because of the work required to keep the clothing clean, also brought about an unsuspected response. As respectability had generally been associated with wearing mats or various forms of woven covering around the hips, the association of plain white clothing with the white barkcloth worn by commoners meant that a woven fibre waist-ornament, either in the form of a mat or a crocheted apron, was worn over white dress material to maintain the status of the nobility.

The work of the anthropologist Ping-Ann Addo in Tonga provides ample evidence that indigenous unstitched cloth, such as fine mats embellished with red parrot feathers or painted and printed barkcloths (*ngatu*), has continued to be associated with the state of the soul, the sacred Tongan polity and the health of the body, despite the availability of stitched clothing and the ready appropriation of stitching and sewing skills for the production of appliqué quilts. While a sumptuary law passed by the missionaries in 1875 outlawed the wearing of painted barkcloth and restricted its production to one day a week, mat-weaving has remained relatively unrestricted – possibly because the Methodist missionaries saw it as a 'work of patience', capable of teaching men and women control over their hands and bodies (and practice for their training in sewing, which would then provide them with clothing).

Regardless of religious or political convictions, these days Tongans consider it a point of pride to wear barkcloth, decorated mats and printed cottons worn tightly wrapped, or casually draped, or as stitched clothing over dresses. More than anything else, the Tongans of the twenty-first century wear a short waist mat (*ta'ovala*) wrapped around the midriff and fastened with a braided cord at the waist. It is these wraps that have become synonymous with a notion of clothing that, in Tonga, alludes to wrapping and layering. Ping-Ann Addo describes the metaphoric potential of such 'covering', which overlays one's other clothing, as extending to the practice of covering freshly slaughtered pig or taro in order to bake it in an earth oven. 'Certain *ta'ovala*', she reports, 'are indeed "baked"; for example, *ta'ovala lokeha* [a type of woven mat worn around the waist] are customarily soaked in seawater and then buried in the ashes of burnt lime coral to give a yellowish tint to the light brown fibres, which are soft to the touch and acquire a smoky smell.'

While in diaspora communities the wearing of mats as formal dress has become limited to ceremonial and festive occasions, imitations of barkcloth in cotton have now been embraced as an outward expression of patriotism towards a distant homeland. Cotton and viscose imitations of Tongan-style barkcloth, printed with distinctive motifs made with *kupesi* pattern boards (design tablets for printing barkcloth), are commissioned by Fijian-Indian traders, who have them printed in Japan for the fabric shops of Auckland's outdoor markets. Through these designs, cotton has surreptitiously become a Pacific material that will be worn as readily by foreigners for an island-style wedding as it is by Tongans, who consider it to be an appropriate form of dress if layered with a waist mat or waist ornaments.

In contemporary Pacific Island life, the missionary-led styles also continue to undergo profound changes. The 'Mother Hubbard' dress has been adapted to numerous local styles known as 'island dress'. Indeed, in Vanuatu, for example, island dresses are no longer regarded as coming from outside but have become an integral part of local *kastom* ('identity'). In order to create variation in pre-fabricated dress patterns, island women select fabric by its colour and quality and seek to control details of the decorations of the dresses. As a result, island dresses are very commonly decorated with binding, ribbons and lace or, at the very least, with pleats folded into the fabric itself. In some parts of southern Vanuatu the patterns plaited into fibres are specific to kin groups; now, as pattern in ready-made bought cloth cannot be controlled, decorative additions such as pinned handkerchiefs are incorporated. More recently, with a rising urban population that is dressing for work in tight skirts, shoes with heels and make-up, the island dress has been relegated from a national icon to a symbol of rural and island-based conservatism. In Vanuatu, young women have begun to wear loose and wide trousers, similar to culottes, that allow for mobility and comfort;

Above, from left to right: Stanley Numalo and Take Chilia wait to be married, Mele village, Efate, Vanuatu, 2004; women sing at a wedding, Mele, Efate, Vanuatu, 2004; Nalkutan dance group assembled at the Celebration for Women, Port Vila, Efate, Vanuatu, 2004; two women dressed for an occasion, Mele village, Efate, Vanuatu, 2004.

Overleaf: Embroidery prepared mainly by Tapuaki Manogi Inavave Mahakitau Vaha, West Auckland, New Zealand, 2004. The imagery draws on local flowers and motifs and is embroidered on pillow cases.

From left to right: Pandanus toy pram made by Niuean weaver Kumisifa Malo Sipeli Tulisi, Auckland, New Zealand, 2004; shopping basket made from flax and pandanus by the Niuean weaver Kumisifa Malo Sipeli Tulisi, Auckland, New Zealand, 2004. Icons of European domesticity are transformed into icons of Pacific modernity through the use of fibre.

in the Cook Islands in eastern Polynesia, however, young women prefer wide shorts for similar reasons.

The Hawaiian *holokû*, which originated in 1820 as an adaptation of an American day gown, is another example of the way sewing facilitated the translation of ideas of status and occasion into material forms that have outlived their colonial past. First adopted by Hawaiian queens, then worn by Hawaiian women as everyday wear, the *holokû* is now formal wear for ritual and festive events celebrating local identity. Hawaii is unique in its ethnic diversity, in large part because of the importation of plantation labourers in the mid to late nineteenth century. Its population, in which no one ethnic group is in the majority, is today primarily differentiated by the length of time the inhabitants have been on the islands. Those born in Hawaii are referred to as *Kama'aina*, meaning old-timers, and they are the ones who continue to wear the *holokû* to events where references to the past are an integral part of affirming status and belonging.

Before the arrival of American Congregationalist missionaries in 1820, Hawaiian women wore a *pa'u* constructed by felting fibres from barkcloth. Each layer of barkcloth was about three to four metres long and about one metre wide. This stiff material was wrapped several times around the waist – the higher the status, the greater the number of layers. Hawaiian queens wore as many as ten layers, and appear to have pressed for the substitution of calico for barkcloth when the thriving sandalwood trade, beginning in 1810, facilitated access to Western textiles. However, it was the latest fashions of 1819 – with their high waists, narrow skirts and long, tight sleeves – worn by the wives of the arriving missionaries that impressed Hawaiian royalty most. The missionary wives, eager to comply in order to secure permission to stay on the island, submitted to requests of

Queen Kalakua and adapted their high-waisted dress style to a loose and comfortable fit, using fabric from the Queen's stores of brocades, silks and chintz. The chiefly class readily adopted the resulting dress-style, but it took many more years before commoners, who initially made the *holokû* out of barkcloth, could trade labour and wood planking for fabric for their wives. By the time photography arrived in Hawaii in the 1860s, everyone wore a *holokû*. In the late nineteenth century, a new fitted style of the *holokû* developed alongside the looser fit, and both are worn to this day, according to the latest fashion.

As in Hawaii, other island nations of eastern Polynesia had long associated the wearing of upper-body garments with status. Museum collections document the importance of so called *tiputa*, 'ponchos' made of barkcloth, which were worn widely across Tahiti and the Cook Islands, together with feathered cloaks and felted capes. It was arguably the layered garments – shirts, waistcoats and jackets – worn by the explorer Captain James Cook, and by the merchants and missionaries who followed his route, that may have persuaded Polynesians of the power of stitched clothing (which could be further harnessed by adopting Christianity).

But it would be a mistake to assume that it was just clothing that was inspired by the arrival of cloth. Home furnishings – such as pillow covers, throws, bedspreads, as well as wall hangings – have been produced by women all over the Pacific. These furnishings share a tenuous relation with European furnishings, but at the same time transpose local motifs and patterns on to the fabrics.

In Niue, embroidered pillow covers of variegated thread capture floral designs produced with cross-stitch patterns which have become a favourite gift item and local treasure. Embroidery, rather than printing, adds depth and weight to the fabric surface, especially when crocheted doilies are incorporated into the design. As ribbons and lace denote localized transpositions of missionary-inspired dress, so too are island identities marked out by the selective uptake and transformation of home furnishings.

Pacific embroideries instantly remind us of European pattern books and embroidery sets which were iconic of Victorian industrial productivity and the rising importance of the home as a place of comfort and rest. Armed with strong notions of the value of the domestic, missionaries made attempts to transpose these ideals on to Pacific Island cultures by imposing them on local people. However, Pacific cultures surpassed their own expectations by transforming the home into elaborately decorated spaces that located productivity and value firmly inside the home, rather than in a separate sphere that existed in industrial Europe. For that reason, pattern books and embroidery sets are the tangible markers of the ownership of production, resources and value in modern Pacific life.

Although early anthropologists and many ethnographic museums shunned them as inauthentic indigenous technology, Polynesian quilting is now subject to major exhibitions in art galleries and museums in New Zealand and Australia. Just as certain fabrics, patterns and dress styles – including the *tivaivai*, the *holokû*, the Tongan *ta'ovala*, the island dress and the *meri bilaus* – are vital to Pacific expatriates seeking out cloth fashions for the re-affirmation of their 'islandness', quilting asserts the relevance of Pacific Island culture to Pacific Islanders.

# Fashioning Modernity

In 1994, when the assertiveness of New Zealand's Polynesian migrant community was becoming more visible, photo shoots organized by a group of expatriate Pacific Islanders, who became known as the 'Pacific Sisters', helped to develop people's awareness of Polynesian culture in New Zealand. Fashion parades, like the Pasifika fashion shows of the 1990s, brought together designers producing feather and barkcloth jewelry, and utilized them in costuming and performance. These inspired young urban artists to attempt to relearn traditional skills, such as plaiting eight-ply strands or preparing and threading *pu'a* (carob) seeds, at a time when 'most people were only thinking about getting hold of the next pair of Nikes', as Pacific artist Rosanna Raymond put it.

Right: Woman wearing *holokû* dress in Hawaii. The *holokû* originated in 1820 as an adaptation of an American day gown. First adopted by Hawaiian queens, then worn by Hawaiian women as everyday wear, the *holokû* is now formal wear for ritual and festive events celebrating local identity.

New materials were incorporated into contemporary fashion designs that bore a conspicuous resemblance to the line and the frond effects of traditional fibre arts. As, according to Polynesian beliefs, the wearing of traditional clothing requires one to demonstrate respect for its *kaupapa* (its cultural foundations and value) through movement and performance, the eclectic mix of the traditional and the new in fashioning Pacific modernity required the deliberate use of irony.

Pacific fashion has been revitalized through the work of these Pacific fashion activists, but it is also apparent that Euro-American fashion design plays a significant part in inspiring dress design for Pacific women. The Samoan two-piece dress (*puletasi*) modelled on the twin set is a striking example of how European fashion has been translated into a visual icon of 'being Samoan'. Italian fashion shops in the cosmopolitan centres of the Pacific and North America as well as glossy magazines with the latest designs are eagerly scanned and are considered a rich resource from which to create new dresses for work or special occasions. The cut, the stitch and the look are literally carried 'in the mind' as women modify what they have seen as they work at home on lengths of cloth with their scissors and Singer sewing machine.

Even away from the urban centres of New Zealand or Australia, there are many occasions at which Pacific Island fashion asserts itself: from the Festival of Pacific Arts, which is held every four years in a variety of locations across the Pacific, to the many local island festivals that are established parts of the calendar.

Other, less obviously marked, occasions for dress-making are sporting competitions, which are taken extremely seriously across the Pacific. The year that was once divided into gardening cycles now undergoes a seasonal cycle of sports that regulate the rhythm of activities across the Pacific Islands. In the Cook Islands,

for instance, June is the tennis season: villagers are out from dawn until the start of the school or working day, and then again from 4 p.m. till dusk, pounding the ball across tarmac netball courts to prepare for intra- and inter-village competitions. It is obligatory to wear a different uniform for each type of sport – whether volleyball, rugby, football or golf – and there are also uniforms representing clan, village or island identity.

Every island nation has its own modern ritual space that is used as a museum and an exhibition, assembly and performance centre. Famous Pacific landmarks include the Tjibaou Cultural Centre (New Caledonia), the National Museum and Library (Rarotonga, the Cook Islands), the Vanuatu Culture Centre and the National Museum and Art Gallery (Papua New Guinea). Exhibition openings and performances are a regular feature on every island and are eagerly attended. The wearing of an island dress, cut and sewn in the latest fashion of a *muumuu* (a modern-style 'Mother Hubbard' dress), is a must, and great pride is taken

in selecting the material and the cut to fit the occasion. If children attend such occasions, then the entire family may be kitted out in the same patterned material, in the same manner as villages attending inter-island competitions.

The principal focal points of fashion across island and diaspora communities are, however, the churches. Church is a formal occasion, demanding that the best outfit (in either white or black/blue) be worn for most of the day, both inside and outside the home. The clothes made for church are the only dresses that are worn for a prolonged period, altered occasionally only by the addition of a new hat or crocheted shawl. Today, it is women's work for the church – irrespective of the orientation of religious teachings – that orchestrates the transmission of skills and values pertaining to stitched cloth and clothing. Delegations of women often travel to workshops held in other island nations to learn new needlework and fabric techniques, returning to teach those who stayed at home. In this way, for example,

Preceding pages, left, above: Shirts and dress material on display in the Fare Pare Store, Otahuhu, Auckland, New Zealand, 2004. Printed cloth for sarongs and shirts is imported and sometimes printed on the islands to reflect locally specific patterns.

Preceding pages, left, below: Print detail of hibiscus at the Pasifika Festival, Auckland, New Zealand, 2004.

Preceding pages, right, clockwise from top left: Shirts, Nuku'alofa, Tonga, 2003; cotton Prints, Port Vila market, Efate, Vanuatu, 2004; cotton prints on sarongs, Port Vila market, Efate, Vanuatu, 2004.

Opposite: Fashion shows on Rarotonga, Cook Islands, and in Papeete, Tahiti. Clockwise from top left: Karotaua Terangi Little winning the fashion show with her yellow *muumuu* dress, Tiare Festival, Rarotonga, Cook Islands, 2003; Miss Tahiti contestant, Papeete, in modern cut dress and traditional pattern, Tahiti, 1999; fashion show, Miss Tiare Festival, Rarotonga, Cook Islands, 2003.

Right: Young man wearing Vanuatuan loin mat over shorts, Port Vila, Efate, Vanuatu, 2004. The expensive new sports shoes and white shorts express as much about the association of contemporary attire with wealth as the fibre loin cloth.

Overleaf: Niuean baskets made of packing strip and hats made of plastic bread bags, Auckland, New Zealand, 2004.

screen-printing and rubbing techniques used in Fiji arrived in other parts of the Pacific, to be combined with tie-dying to produce an avalanche of sarongs and other fabrics.

In the contemporary Pacific, the church is the cutting-edge domain for the organization and competitive display of productivity centred on designs in fibre and fabric. Spectacular cloth competitions between the parishes and dioceses of individual islands dominate everyday activity and planning, so forming an integral part of the yearly calendar. The cloth wealth on show on the day of the competition is as visually stunning as it is diverse, ranging from lace to crocheted tablecloths, sarongs, pillow covers and painted or stitched *tivaivai*. As women's workshops are also tied into pan-Pacific arts festivals, there is a great awareness of what is worn or made in which part of the Pacific.

An equally important platform to try out ideas and set new trends is the weekly market. Whether urban or rural, the Pacific market is not only crowded with food stalls selling cooked dishes and raw produce, but also with stalls selling island prints as sarongs, dresses or shirts, along with baskets, hats, jewelry and T-shirts. Both island prints and custom-made T-shirts attract attention from local customers. Every island nation in the Pacific now has its own printing outlet, and new designs are springing up all the time.

## New Materials

Items that appear quite familiar but which, upon closer inspection, look and feel unsettlingly strange are also sold at the markets. What seems at first glance to be something that is mere packaging, a by-product of consumption usually thrown away,

is innovatively revisualized by Pacific women in terms of its colour, its luminosity, its texture as well as more abstractly, by its transformative capacities inherent in the property of the material itself. There are baskets made out of plastic packaging tape in sizes and shapes that befit the Western demand for shopping bags. Flower leis, made out of plastic carrier bags, can be seen hanging from the rafters of stalls, glistening in the sun and rustling in the wind. Certain island nations, such as the Cook Islands and Niue, excel in making hats from raffia and plastics that are very popular, as they come in the gleaming-white, florescent-green or baby-pink colours that are felt to go well with the Sunday best. Elsewhere, Tongan women compete to make innovative woven designs from any accessible materials, weaving them together to make decorative girdles (*kiekie*) worn around the waist. Media range from the inner stem of the giant hibiscus (*fau*), unravelled plastic sacking to lengths of shiny video tape. Other items appear softer and more familiar: cushion covers with pompoms that were crocheted out of unravelled sweaters, or woollen dresses that reached the Pacific as second-hand goods.

Neither new, nor aged, the 'recycled' materials visually coin an 'in-between-ness' with many faces. As Pacific artist Rosanna Raymond has so succinctly expressed it, 'We are all experimenting with the bits and pieces of our past. Recycling has also been particularly important for women who have grown up on tiny coral atolls in the Pacific.' Playful and humorous, a second look at these materials makes you wonder whether they have been made with the dominant white population in urban Australia and New Zealand in mind, as they reveal that they are not what they appear to be. The ironic, self-deprecating references to brand images that have dominated Pacific modernity are returned to the onlooker: like an orange peel, what we are looking at is

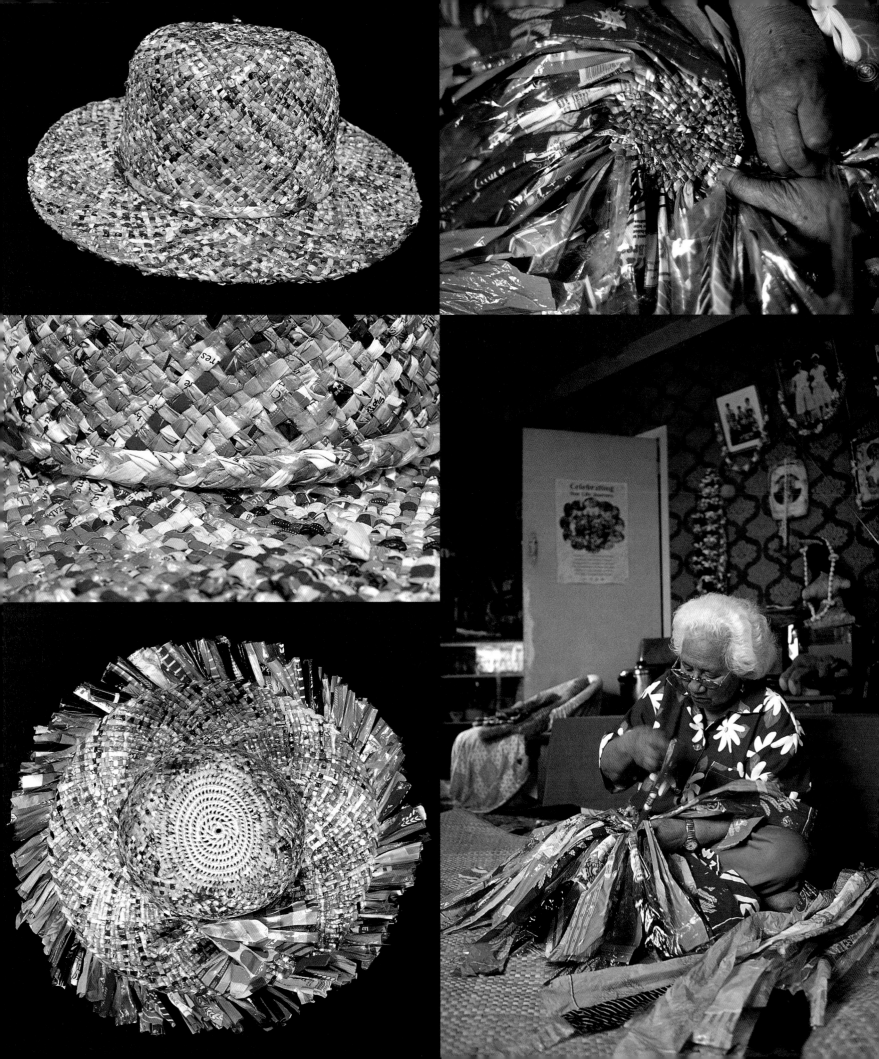

Below: Detail of Tokelau fan made of raffia together with pandanus and coconut leaf spines, Auckland, New Zealand, 2004.

Opposite, clockwise from top left: Raffia hat with coloured trim, Rarotonga, Cook Islands, 2003; raffia hat, Rarotonga, Cook Islands, 2003; raffia hat, Otara, Auckland, New Zealand. 2003.

Overleaf, clockwise from left: Niuean placemat made from raffia woven on to coconut leaf spines, Pasifika Festival, Auckland, New Zealand, 2004; detail of Niuean raffia placemat by Moka Siulani Eveni, Auckland, 2004; Niuean raffia placemat, Pasifika Festival, Auckland, New Zealand, 2004; detail of raffia placemat in Niuean style, Auckland, New Zealand, 2004.

something which has not been consumed; instead it has been transformed into an enduring product traversing conventional boundaries and expectations like art.

It is this spontaneous, public and interactive form, which combines contemporary materials with old techniques of basketry and cordage, that has emerged as a most vibrant visual marker of Pacific modernity. The innovative use of new materials, however, does not undermine the importance of coconut and pandanus leaves in Pacific design. To the contrary, the smooth and

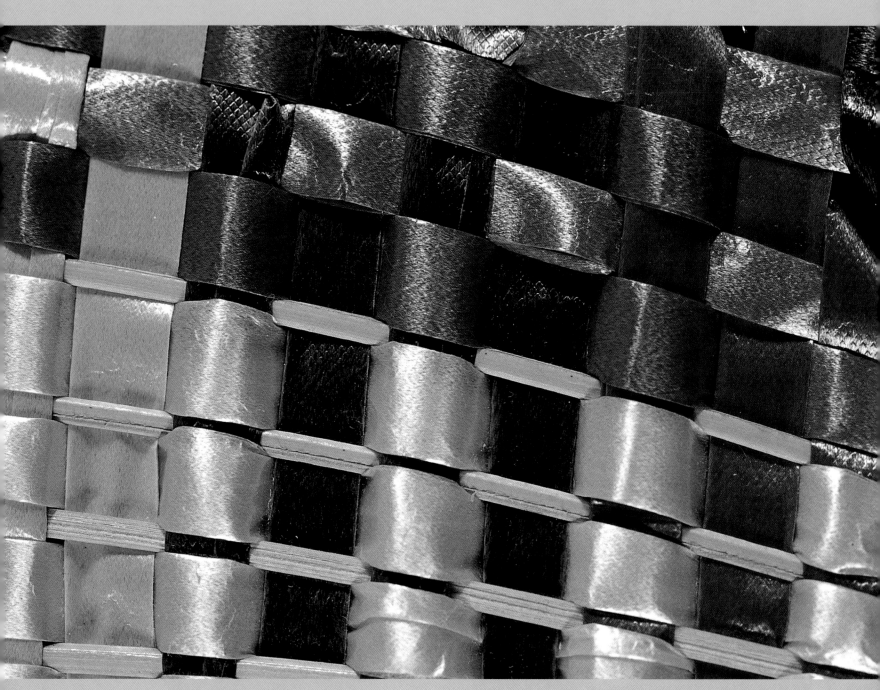

fluorescent surfaces of synthetic materials such as raffia, plastic bread and rice bags, as well as packaging tape, combined with their durability against wear and water, their longevity and their economic value, simulate and reinforce the qualities that make coconut and pandanus so desirable wherever they are available.

In the urban centres of the Pacific, particularly in Auckland, Sydney and Los Angeles, where access to coconut, pandanus and hibiscus is virtually impossible, women rely on networks of relatives living in rural villages to deliver these raw materials, often an aeroplane ride away. Shopping baskets woven from packing materials, place mats made from raffia or plastic bread bags neatly twisted and plaited into colourful hats not only underline the ethos of 'making do' in urban Pacific life but actually reinvigorate one's relationship to roots in the islands of the Pacific which are so heavily invested with ideas of history, genealogy and identity.

Crocheted flowers that adorn the urban house interiors of the Pacific diaspora communities are therefore not just nostalgic reflections, but are actively claiming a brighter future by transforming discarded materials back into images of light and life.

Opposite: Pandanus flowers woven by Niuean weaver Moka Siulani Eveni, Avondale, Auckland, New Zealand, 2004.

Above: Woollen crocheted flowers by Niuean weaver Moka Siulani Eveni, Avondale, Auckland, New Zealand, 2004.

Overleaf, clockwise from left: Dancers from Tuvalu at the 8th Festival of Pacific Arts, Noumea, New Caledonia, 2000; 'Faka Ha'apai', Tongan fine mat embroidered with synthetic decorations distinctive to the island of Ha'apai, Nuku'alofa, Tonga, 2003; detail of 'Faka Ha'apai' mat technique, Nuku'alofa, Tonga, 2003.

# PATTERN IN ARCHITECTURE AND INTERIOR DESIGN

One of the principal uses of fibre art and its pattern was in architecture. Cordage lashed to wooden posts, while lattice-work walls and thatches formed the basis of the exterior shell of the home. In many parts of the Pacific imported materials have superseded the use of fibre, yet interior walls are still covered with fibrous materials – from barkcloth to hats and fans.

When Captain James Cook's *Endeavour* sailed around the Hawaiian archipelago in the eighteenth century, the ship's artist, John Webber, sketched a variety of thatched houses dotted along the coastline. The ship's company could not have known that two hundred years later the same coastline would look akin to that of a Western city. It is not just that modern high-rise buildings have become commonplace in coastal cities in the Pacific; the legacy of colonialism, with its concern for market-led regulation of people's everyday lives, has restructured people's leisure and work, and thereby their living spaces.

The residues of colonial administration can still be seen in the villages and hamlets of the contemporary Pacific, decades after independence was achieved. This is partly because colonial efforts to regulate standards of hygiene, and to formalize identities through taxation and head counts, persist in current-day government initiatives. Administrative standards imposed on households often ignored the very different conceptions of social space among the various cultures of the Pacific. The most far-reaching change imposed was the enforcement of Western burial practices, which led to radical upheavals. While the dead had been buried under the house or on the boundary of individual house sites in certain areas, colonial regulations stipulated they should be placed in village cemeteries located adjacent to the mission, on the village perimeter. It is significant that following independence traditional mortuary practices were resumed once more, wherever possible.

Struggles to reclaim control over living spaces have concentrated on the burial issue: the house in Pacific society is not just conceived as a dwelling, but as an essential harbour of the principle of life. As such, the house acts as a formal ritual space – a symbol of concerns with the social nature of enclosure and the epitomization of hidden, non-public resources. In surveying Pacific architecture, we find a formal architectural emphasis on openings, porches and verandas that accentuates ideas of the permeability of boundaries, as well as internally stratified and impermeable living spaces that tend to echo concerns about the control and flow of life-giving forces, such as light.

If fibre and fabric harness and control the vital principles of light in the Pacific, then the principal use of fibre in the construction of the house has acted as a primary agent in the anchoring of light and life – both in the past and today. Where fibre and fabric allow for the subtle accentuation of degrees of enclosure, prefabricated housing emulates this through the use

Preceding pages, from left: Tree house, British New Guinea, *c.* 1900; cordage rafter lashings woven into criss-cross pattern, fale tonga, Nuku'alofa, Tonga, 1998; tree house, British New Guinea, *c.* 1900.

Above, left: Modern tin roof house, Viti Levu, Fiji, 1998.

Below, left: Traditional Fijian thatched house called *bure, c.* 1900.

Opposite, above: 'Mourning and dead house at Kalo, British New Guinea', Papuan Gulf Region, photographed by J. W. Lindt, late nineteenth century.

Opposite, below: Village scene, Port Moresby, Papua New Guinea, photographed by J. W. Lindt, late nineteenth century.

of architectural features such as the porch, the door, shutters, louvres and curtains.

## House, Growth and Life

Corrugated tin roofs, prefabricated bricks and panels are much in use in the contemporary Pacific house. In the urban centres of the Pacific, Pacific Islanders share the same semi-detached houses as the rest of the multicultural society. Take Port Moresby, Papua New Guinea's sprawling capital: most people live in wood and breezeblock buildings constructed from materials imported from Australia; in Hanuabada, on the other hand, Port Moresby's coastal suburb, people retain a sense of the past with houses built along the shoreline and raised upon wooden stilts, as they were in the pre-contact era. Yet we may be mistaken in concluding that the former is a more modern living space than the latter.

Away from the urban centres, we find that many Pacific Islanders still prefer to rely on traditional architectural styles and materials. Even though modern tools such as chainsaws, chisels and nails may be used, building construction utilizes natural materials from the local environment such as tropical woods, bamboo canes, lashings from locally produced cordage as well as leaf foliage from trees and plants. While in coastal regions of south-eastern Papua New Guinea many traditional houses are built on stilts, in other parts of the Pacific (such as in Fiji) houses are constructed on rock mounds. We also find that many houses are built on the beach or in the forest, anchored by long wooden posts driven into the ground.

Pacific Islanders are fully aware of the benefits of the abundant, locally available materials, both in an economic and practical sense: these building materials grow naturally and provide a more comfortable living environment than modern materials. There are clearly many practical benefits in using plant materials in a hot and humid climate, where gas and electricity supplies are not always available. A thatched roof facilitates cooking on an open fire inside the house, just as a house with no walls enables people to gather freely inside and disperse without hindrance.

Given our inclination to foreground the functional role of a building, we could be forgiven for assuming that walls and roofs –

the outer skin of a house – simply offer protection from the outside elements. Yet these are the most important design elements in Pacific architecture, as they help formalize activities within and around the house.

One place where architectural diversity is well documented is Hawaii. John Webber's sketches on the *Endeavour* with Cook depict a variety of architectural styles in eighteenth-century Hawaii: some featuring buildings raised on piles, some lacking walls, some with gabled, straight roofs and others with curved roofs.

Still in the mid-twentieth century, work on the material culture of the Hawaiian islands divides traditional architectural design in Hawaii into four main types: those without walls, those with stone walls, those with walls and gabled roof, and those with walls and hipped roof. The simplest form of design was the building without walls. Requiring the minimum of effort to construct, this was built with a basic framework of posts driven into the ground. The frame consisted of two main vertical posts secured to a ridgepole, from which the remaining rafters were lashed together at the ends. Buildings made with stone walls were constructed in a similar way, though with a base of stones

113

Left: Thatched round house, Lifou village, New Caledonia, 1998.

Below: Detail of a thatched house under construction highlighting the lattice-work design of the walls, lashed together by cordage, Tanna, Vanuatu, 1998.

Opposite, left: Traditional *bure* house built on stone platform with thatched roof and patterned façade, Tobu village, Viti Levu, Fiji, 1998.

Opposite, right: Traditional *bure* house under construction, showing the rafters bound in a lattice-work structure, Ba village, Viti Levu, Fiji, 1998.

that provided a more stable structure. Stones were easily located and piled to form four walls, and a wooden framework was erected on top of this. Similar houses called *bure* continue to be built in Fiji today.

Buildings with gables and hipped roofs were more complex in their design and required skilled labourers to erect them. Their design relied on the construction of a wooden framework consisting of corner posts, wall posts, ridge posts, a ridgepole, rafters and gable posts. The wooden posts were prepared with notches to maximize stability, and lashed together using a three-ply braid of a local variety of grass or, occasionally, coconut-husk fibre. The gabled-roof buildings were used at the time of Cook's voyages, while the hipped-roof house – with its gabled end tilted inwards and upwards – resulted from later European influence.

Thatching added character, and both techniques and materials varied from island to island. Interesting designs of interlacing patterns were created using leaf fibres, which were anchored to a wooden framework with a type of cordage. In Hawaii, the thatching technique relied on bunches of thatch being tied to horizontal poles on the roof and walls using three-ply cord.

Hawaiians preferred to use a special type of grass (*pili*) because of its aromatic qualities and its colour, although in some islands pandanus and sugar cane leaves were used as alternatives. Both the pandanus and sugar cane leaves were soaked in the sea (to soften them) before being tied into the horizontal thatches.

According to Buck's observations, the final thatches placed along the ridge of the house (those closest to the ridge) were the most intricate and entailed carrying out a special ritual for those involved in house construction. The narrow opening between the final two thatches along the top ridge was covered up with additional grass. This was secured with an extra pole, laid over the top of the existing ridgepole, from which extra layers of thatch were laid. On completing the thatched roof, the thatch was trimmed. The thatch on either side of the door was plaited in a check design, as were the four corners.

The boundaries of these houses, both the exterior and the interior walls, were created using woven leaf fibres. These woven partitions resembled upturned mats and helped segregate the inner domestic space of the house from the outside world of danger, sorcery and malevolent spirits. In a more practical sense, woven walls offered privacy from neighbours as well as protection from the weather. Take Manihiki in the Cook Islands: there, the houses were built with thatched roofs, although the wooden structure differed somewhat from the design of the Hawaiian house. Inside the house one would have seen palm-leaf wall-screens tied to the posts of the house. The walls were constructed by plaiting coconut palm fronds and resembled sitting mats.

Fibre wall dividers are still used occasionally. The technique for plaiting fibre follows the pattern for mat-making, although the whole coconut palm leaf is used to make a wall screen. The fronds from one side of the leaf lead, while those from the

opposite side are folded over the midrib. The fronds are then plaited together to make a continuous patterned surface and, where spaces appear, extra leaf fronds are introduced into the plaiting surface. The plaiting technique can be altered slightly to make interesting visual effects with the palm fronds. Variations in the woven surface are made possible by changing the order in which the left-hand fronds pass over the right-hand fronds. The far edge of the screen is finished off using a braiding technique, and then the end is knotted.

In a similar fashion, houses in the Solomon Islands and New Ireland today still feature thatched roofs of sago palm, pandanus or coconut palm, woven on to a lattice frame of horizontal poles. The most striking features of many houses from this region are the plaited walls that combine light and dark elements to give a geometric effect. These highly decorative façades are made from strips of bamboo, interlaced into various patterns. The varying patterns feature the names of particular flora and fauna. Moreover, in Island Melanesia we may infer that patterned façades are a means to project social identity – much of the material culture produced in this region exhibits similar patterns in which slight variations differentiate between local clans.

We can now begin to imagine how the exterior appearance of the house can take on the form of a plaited mat or woven basket. Just as mats and baskets are produced in a breathtaking array of shapes and sizes, Webber's sketches of Hawaiian architecture remind us that buildings too come in many different forms that are used in various contexts. What then, we may ask, does this diversity in design achieve, and what, if any, is the significance attached to using fibrous materials in creating the outside layer of the house? To begin to answer this question we should examine the ideas that underlie architectural design in the Pacific.

Preceding pages: Detail of the lattice-work structure of a roof, with rafters lashed with cordage, Lifou village, New Caledonia, 1998.

Opposite, left: Patterned wall interior of a traditional *bure*. The patterns are made using flattened bamboo strips reversed in places to add contrast, Tobu village, Viti Levu, Fiji, 1998.

Opposite, right: Interior scene of a traditional house, highlighting the lengths of sago palm thatch woven on to a pole, Marovo Lagoon, Solomon Islands, 1998. Patterned walls of traditional houses are an inherent structural component.

Right: Sago palm thatch house built on stilts, Guadalcanal, Solomon Islands, 1998.

Below: Interior living space of sago palm house with traditional geometric patterns decorating the wall space, Marovo Lagoon, Solomon Islands, 1998.

House design, by its very nature, enforces separation between those staying outside and those who remain inside. Either with walls and thatch, or wooden planks and corrugated iron, the enclosed space provides a place to hide, the opportunity to be reclusive and to stay safely away from prying eyes. Woven trellis walls, patterned bamboo façades or sweeping thatched roofs obscure the dark and dimly lit interior spaces hidden within. Small doorways, shutters or openings offer little invitation to the would-be visitor. In essence, all these attributes of Pacific houses operate to restrict or prevent the flow of movement from one place to another, sometimes enhanced by protective woven devices such as the *timbuwara* in the Highlands of Papua New Guinea.

When examining the design of the Pacific home, it is pertinent to highlight the way the spatial separation between the exterior and interior plays upon the duality of existence within Pacific ritual – that is, the nocturnal, dangerous and uncultivated exterior, the source of light and life, and the interior, where light is transformed into life-giving substance. While walls may be commonly perceived as barriers that separate the outside from the inside, Pacific fibre houses point to the inverse conception: walls act as permeable passages that can variably contain and harness as well as release life-giving forces such as light.

The significance of the patterned and permeable wall is very much at the heart of architectural design and the use of the house in the Pacific. In Melanesia, the dark interior of houses is largely devoid of decorations and furnishings; indeed, there are expressions likening it to the womb. This interior space is carefully ordered, swept clean every day, with possessions kept neatly on the wooden rafters overhead. The ethnobotantist H. B. Guppy, visiting the eastern Solomon Islands in the late nineteenth century, made detailed remarks about interior house designs there. He laments the lack of house decoration – both internal and external – most probably because he observed the richness in decoration on artefacts such as spears, paddles and shields. He does, however, mention that rows of pig jaws, fish skeletons and the dried skins of flying foxes hang from the roof above the entrance. Fishing implements, spears and clubs are placed in the rafters of the house, though there is little in the way of furniture except for some mats, a cooking pot and a stone hearth in the centre of the floor.

Not only should we be wary of assuming that interiors are lavishly designed, but we should also be cautious in thinking that the house is the domestic sphere of women. The house stands empty during the day, with the fruits of women's work concentrated outside the inner space of the house; women spend the day in their gardens, on the rocky reefs hunting for shellfish or attending church meetings. Even when women are not working in their gardens or fishing on the reef, they may sit around in the shady spots near the porch of a house, or in the shade of a tree with other women, surrounded by bundles of dried leaves, producing baskets, mats or fans as they exchange stories with one another.

In stark contrast to the dormant feel of the house during the day, the woven walls and plaited thatches of Pacific houses come alive in the evenings, when people return to their houses to eat and sleep. An example of the relation between the work of gardening and ideas that inform the design of houses is taken from New Ireland in Island Melanesia. Here, the garden is a place for the growth of root vegetables and plants, which the interior design of the house complements by transforming the products of gardening into the seeds of life inside a large stone oven, situated at the centre of an open-plan house, which is lit upon every return from the gardens to cook root crops wrapped in bundles of banana leaf. The relation between the house and the garden is further apparent in the periodic rotation of garden space and house space: new houses are built on old gardens, while abandoned house sites are burnt down and the cleared land cultivated for gardening.

In New Ireland, houses consist of wooden framed buildings, with split bamboo cane walls and sago palm thatch. After a rectangular frame is erected in a village hamlet, flattened

Above: *Timbuwara*, a protective door decoration from the Highlands of Papua New Guinea.

Opposite: from top (1) to bottom (4): (1) Framework of a traditional house, consisting of poles and cordage lashings, Port Vila, Efate, Vanuatu, 1997. (2) Interior walls and shutters of a traditional house, highlighting the lattice-work structure with woven sago palm thatch, Marovo Lagoon, Solomon Islands, 1998. (3) Building a cane house, Port Vila, Efate, Vanuatu, 2004. Patterned façades are a common feature of houses in Melanesia and are related to both their structural properties as well as symbolic connotations. (4) Two men making panels for a cane house, Efate, Vanuatu, 2004.

bamboo strips are nailed to it to form the walls. The roof is rather more complex: the leaves of the sago palm are cut down and dried. They are then sewn on to a lattice frame to make a form of thatch. These thatches are tied or nailed on to the main frame of the house to create a pitched roof, providing a run-off for rainwater and, at the same time, allowing the sea breeze to ventilate the interior space.

The interior of the house is largely empty, with the exception of the stone oven, a small hearth opposite the main doorway, shelves for pots and plates and woven mats leaning against the walls of the house. People refer to this dark interior space with words that resonate with ideas of self-fashioning – words that refer to the womb of a childbearing woman, to the spring of a stream in the forest, and to the clouds of smoke that billow through the thatched roofing whenever the stone oven is lit. It is when the smoke of the lit oven streams through the roof of the house that we can see the transformation of the products of light into the things that make life possible, such as the serving of cooked food.

There are many houses used exclusively for cooking and sleeping in this way. Spatial organization is rigidly adhered to, so we find that sleeping areas are kept quite separate between the sexes. Widows and unmarried women of all ages sleep together in one house, while men of a marriageable age sleep together in another building. Married couples have their own quarters. These principles are enforced due to the importance placed on everyday ideas of avoidance and respect that entail a degree of spatial separation between men and women, as well as between some men. Thus the design of houses, with their fibrous exteriors, separates the sexes when families come together at the end of the day.

Overleaf: Sago palm leaves are carefully woven on to a longitudinal strip which, when assembled, protects against the elements, while allowing air circulation, Efate, Vanuatu, 2004.

Pages 124–125: The dark interior spaces of vast thatched men's houses in the Papuan Gulf were the abode of spirits where they were temporarily captured and turned into creative and life-giving forces harnessed by initiated men.

## Men's Houses in Melanesia

By far the most important architectural feature in Melanesian society is the men's house. These often large and imposing buildings serve as ritual spaces for initiated men. Within these grand structures men may discuss ritual knowledge secretly, a discreet distance away from those who may overhear. Entry to the men's house is for members only; membership involves some form of initiation ceremony, a dramatic experience resulting in the imparting of secret knowledge from the initiated to the new initiates. Women are generally excluded from men's houses and, as a result, this space is often a seat of male ritual and political power.

The design of the men's house facilitates the containment of spiritual power. For it is the men's house, with its dense, fibrous outer skin, that acts as the centre of ritual activity in village life and as an enclosure for the temporary containment of invisible forces deemed to harbour life-giving properties. The construction of a men's house, with the growth of its fibrous exterior skin, is carefully timed to coincide with ritual activities that attempt to seize and control spiritual forces spatially located elsewhere.

A good example of a men's house using traditional fibre materials is found in the Papuan Gulf where huge ceremonial men's houses (*eravo*) belonging to the Elema people were once made of wooden posts with a dense thatch outer skin. The buildings, sometimes over 100 feet (30 metres) in length, rose up some 50 feet (15 metres) at the front, before sloping down along the ridge to a height of only 12 feet (4 metres). The dense leaf thatch covering the roof and a coconut leaf barrier obscured the activities inside, adding to their mystery. The design of the *eravo* resembled a huge monster, its mouth a vast opening to its dark inner entrails. Yet the doorway did not provide simple passageway, as a fibrous barrier of coconut palm leaves tied to a wooden framework obscured the interior and, in so doing, restricted the flow of people into and out of this huge structure.

This vast thatch edifice once harboured life-giving forces that were responsible for the continued well-being of their communities. In order for the community to flourish, sea and forest spirits would be lured inside the belly of the *eravo*, even as it was being constructed, and contained within an assemblage of carvings such as brightly painted, oval-shaped *hohoa* boards.

The beats of drums, the rattle of shells and the shrill notes of trumpets drifting out of the *eravo* at night would alert the village women of the spirits' presence. Once the house was finished, a special ceremony would signal the completion of its growth. Masked men would burst out of the thatched structure from a specially constructed side entrance. These specially initiated men wore conical masks constructed from fibres and cane, which resembled the elongated form of the *eravo* itself. Other masks worn for mortuary feasts were the mythical offspring of the life force believed to reside within the *eravo*, a force that originally lived in the sea before being lured into the thatched building at night.

The idea that buildings are living, growing edifices for the containment of life force is as relevant to societies in Melanesia now as it was then. The building of fibre houses is usually timed to coincide with ceremonies marking new stages in life, such as marriages, deaths and initiation rites. Just as a person's skin dries and wrinkles with age, so do the outer skins of buildings, metaphorically, as the leaf fibres gradually degrade, reaching a state of disrepair before finally falling apart. In this sense, Melanesian houses are symbolic of the growth and decay of the body. Ramshackle buildings that were once homes to people who are now deceased litter village hamlets. Many of these are set aflame, along with the person's belongings, in a special ceremony to rid the space of any remnants of the former resident's life force.

## Ritual Space in Polynesia

In Polynesia, attempts to harness and contain life force very much come into play throughout the range of architectural designs. In comparison to Melanesia, in Polynesian architectural design the primary purpose of walls and thatches is to hinder and contain the flow of these invisible forces. As a membrane that envelops those inside, woven walls protect them from the threat of exposure to invisible forces that may emanate from high- or low-ranking persons passing close to the house.

In eastern Polynesia (Tahiti and the Society Islands, for instance) houses – especially their size and shape – reflected the rank of the owner. People used numerous houses for a variety of purposes: sleeping, cooking, washing, canoe storage and barkcloth-making. Special temples were even constructed to house objects of heightened sanctity such as god staffs, which were once worshipped on the island of Rarotonga. In New Zealand, large meeting houses continue to be constructed with elaborate carved façades invoking images of Maori ancestral deities.

Oval-shaped and rectangular houses were built with sloping roofs and gables. Wooden frames were constructed using rudimentary joins and then lashed together with cordage of various colours. Thatched roofs of coconut or pandanus leaves were commonly used, while walls were made from strips of bamboo placed vertically. Walls were nonexistent in some houses, although occasionally woven mats were used as moveable partitions.

Where once thatched patterns captured the eye, now neatly arranged hats, wedding photographs and training certificates mark the aspirations of the household. The modern Polynesian house, although using materials such as plasterboard and breezeblock, retains the style of a formal interior space. Randomly placed hats, fans and mats, as well as crocheted tablecloths, quilted cushions and bedspreads, adorn the interior walls, floors and furnishings of the modern home, providing lasting reminders of ties to relatives who once gifted these most precious things. Hanging next to these are photographs, certificates and mementos of significant events in the life of the household.

Here, the richly decorated walls reveal the spiritual importance of containment in transforming icons of growth into the accumulation of wealth.

Whereas traditional houses were generally made up of fibres and foliage in eastern Polynesia, the architecture of religious monuments relied upon the use of stone blocks. These stone edifices, known as *marae* in Tahiti and the Society Islands, were constructed from stones trimmed into regular shapes and arranged to form an enclosure. Surrounded by a low rectangular wall, the interior space was generally paved, with columns of stone rising up to form a stepped platform. Within the *marae* stood carved wooden deities depicting human figures, as well as carved posts symbolizing animals, birds and fish. During ceremonial occasions many of these carvings were covered with garlands, plant fibres and strips of barkcloth. The practice of enclosing the *marae* and wrapping the images housed inside acted to contain and control life-giving forces.

Whether performed with stone or with fibre wrappers, the enclosure of space was a central tenet for the containment of life force in Polynesia. It is within the stone enclosures of *marae* that chiefs were inaugurated as divine mediators between the gods and the people. Low-ranking people in Polynesian society risked sickness by coming within close proximity of these high-ranking chiefs due to the powerful life force believed to exude from their bodies. In turn, a chief's power could diminish should he come too close to low-ranking people. In a similar manner to the enclosing of the *marae*, the chief's *mana* was primarily controlled through a process of wrapping, in which high-ranking men covered themselves in layers of barkcloth or fibre mats in order to control the flow of life force.

Opposite: God staff, Rarotonga, Cook Islands, early nineteenth century. Wooden representations of gods, wrapped in barkcloth, were worshipped in pre-contact Polynesia.

Below: Maori door lintel carved from wood, mid-nineteenth century. The lintel would have been placed above the doorway demarcating an area of sacred space inside a meeting house. The meeting house is a focus for Maori pride and often built competitively.

Overleaf: Church and people at school in Fagani, San Christobal, Solomon Islands, c. 1900. Traditional patterns cover the building's façade, marking out a new space for religious worship.

## Church Architecture

We can learn a lot about the principle of enclosure in relation to architectural design by studying the design of local Christian missions in the Pacific. During the nineteenth century, the region became a hive of activity for evangelical missionaries, who were eager to take the Word of God to islanders and to extend the Christian community by converting entire populations. European missionaries established bases in Polynesia – for instance, in Tahiti and Samoa – before moving into Melanesia, where they sometimes set up mission stations with the aid of converted Polynesians.

What eventually emerged was a marked change in village life. Village communities, originally orientated towards ritual activities, were transformed by new regimes of labour and church activity dictated to by the missionaries. These activities often centred round the mission station, a makeshift building erected in the centre of a village. It was from here that missionaries began their quest to convert the rural populations.

Christian missions became the new ritual spaces for Pacific Islanders. To emphasize their importance, church architecture was

often designed to resemble traditional architecture in its highly localized forms. In the Solomon Islands, the façades of the mission stations were covered in traditional pattern systems, although glass windows were incorporated. Missionaries stipulated that local converts should appear for worship clothed, as naked people were deemed unfit for prayer and offended European sensibilities. In New Ireland, highly localized designs appeared in mission architecture after the arrival of the Methodist and Catholic missions at the end of the nineteenth century. The interiors of many missions displayed traditional designs, such as geometric patterns and shapes, and in this way retained a local sense of ancestrality.

Church architecture in the Cook Islands, on the other hand, differs radically from the old ritual spaces created for the worship of gods. Churches are built from limestone covered in an array of bright colours and feature an interior design not unlike that of any Western church. Yet it is the world of light and life that we are reminded of when walking into these places.

The brightly lit interior space, the colourful patterns and whitewashed floors and walls give off a potent life-giving luminosity. The members of the congregation, dressed in formal black, cover themselves in plaited mats so as to control the potential contagion of this invisible form of energy.

The role of fibre in architectural design is to orchestrate and essentially control orifices and openings into and out of the inner space, thereby regulating the permeability of the enclosure. Rather than being a superfluous decoration of architectural structure, fibre patterns were and continue to be a fundamental part of built design. In containing and transforming the principles of life – through the harnessing of light – Pacific architecture resonates with ideas that are commonly associated with the social body. It is this quality of the use of fibre in architecture to contain, while revealing, which alludes to its inherent conception as a second skin and thus brings it into the parameters of the body politic.

Preceding pages: St Martin's Roman Catholic Church at Tenaru, Guadalcanal, Solomon Islands, 1998. Church architecture often bears the hallmarks of traditional designs, suggesting the accommodation of Christianity into local religious forms.

With the advent of Christianity, the church became the new space for ritual activity, displacing the men's houses and associated cult activities. The image bottom right is a detail of the patterned façade, showing the cross alongside traditional pattern systems.

Opposite: 'An Ysabel Church'. Church and congregation in the Solomon Islands with sago leaf thatch roofing laid out in the foreground, c. 1900.

Top, left: 'Island shrine', sacred ground, Solomon Islands, c. 1900.

Top, right: 'Islet shrine, Tendas, Vella Lavella, Solomon Islands', c. 1900.

Above: 'Memorial Cross, the Christian Pioneer of Guadalcanal, Maravovo', Solomon Islands, c. 1900.

Opposite, above left: Sago palm Church, Tamale village, Honiara, Solomon Islands, 1998. The lattice-work structure of the church design is constructed using traditional methods. Wall panels are easily removed to aid access and to screen off activities inside.

Opposite, above right: Sago palm Church, Tamale village, Honiara,

Solomon Islands, 1998. The interior of the church laid out with aisles. In many churches in Melanesia, the pulpit was often decorated using traditional pattern systems.

Opposite, centre: Saint Louis Church, Fusi, Upolu, Samoa, 1996.

Opposite, bottom: Safotu Church, Savaii, Samoa, 1996.

Below: Sacred Heart of Jesus Church, Upolu, Samoa, 1996. In Polynesia, church interiors are painted white denoting the presence of life-giving forces and spiritual power. As places of ritual worship, church interiors are designed to capture light as a source of life.

Above: Pulpit inside a church constructed using traditional methods, Lotofua, Ha'apai, Tonga, 1998.

Right: Detail of roof construction in a traditional house (fale tonga), Nuku'alofa, Tonga, 1998, highlighting the lattice-work structure, stylized lashings and patterned pillars that permeate Tongan fibre arts.

Overleaf: Detail of traditional fale tonga roof construction, Nuku'alofa, Tonga, 1998. Dyed coconut fibres twisted into cordage are lashed on to house frames to produce an endless number of colourful patterns. These designs have been the inspiration for contemporary artists such as Filipe Tohi, who explores the mathematical implications of cordage patterns in a variety of media.

# PATTERNS

# ON THE BODY

# 5

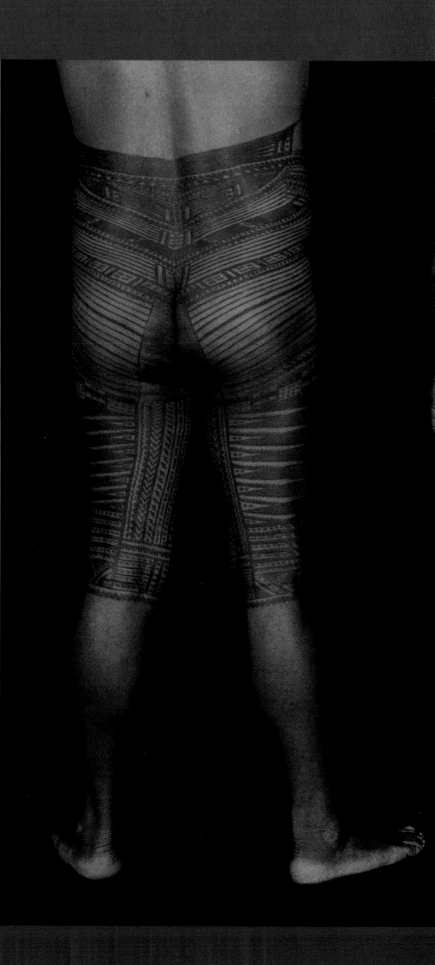

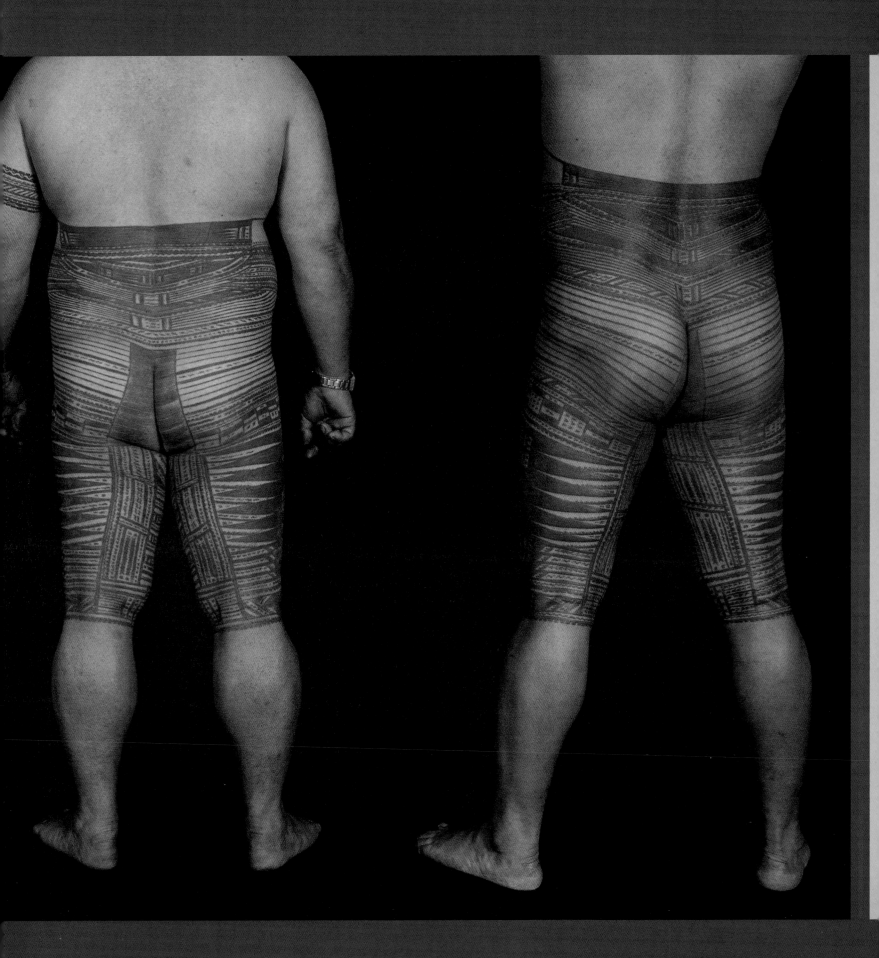

The house and the body are intimately linked in the Pacific. The house is a scaled version of the body and, like a second skin, serves to harness, transform and release life-giving forces. The relation between house and body is not purely abstract, but finds tangible form in the patterns woven into the fibres enveloping both the house and the body. Patterns in fibre on the body – those that are woven, stencilled or painted on to layers that wrap, only to be further covered by feathers, shells or bone – mirror the combination of permeability and buffering attributed to houses. By surrounding the body with layers of patterns in fibre and fabric that exude an impression of relative density beyond the functional, a notion of body comes to the fore that speaks of a surface whose impermanence and superficiality is of profound importance.

In fact, across the Pacific, the word commonly used for body is 'skin', a spatial envelope whose analogue is found in the cultivated land that separates inner spaces teeming with life from those of the forest or the sea that harbour the spirits of the dead. The analogy of the bodily skin with garden land is a telling one, for it suggests that like the garden, which is worked upon for as long as life exists in the villages that live within its reach, the skin needs to be worked upon for life to dwell in the body. By the same token, the membrane of the body – the physical skin – is never of the same consistency for long.

At the high points of sociality and vitality (such as marriage ceremonies or ritual exchanges), greased and perfumed with oil, and having taken in food rich in liquid and fat, the skin is made permeable and, thereby, prepared to give off and absorb light and luminosity in an exchange that renews life at both the level of the person and of society. During times when maintaining distance is paramount, such as during mourning or periods of tension, the skin is hardened with paint substances and with decorations that, like nails, are likened to the hardening substances of the body, in order to create a shield-like constitution that protects and repels. It is on the basis of this logic that ritual representations commemorating the dead find their climax in the symbolic removal of skin, which takes a variety of forms across the Pacific. In ancient Tahiti, it was represented by the ritual unwrapping of a figurative representation of the dead at the height of the ritual of *pai'atua*, 'the gathering of the gods'; in the Marquesas Islands the tattooed skin of a deceased person was physically removed as the final gift to the gods; while in New Ireland this removal of skin today takes the form of an exchange of patterns painted on, and incised in, wooden sculptures representing the dead. Ironically, it is the symbolic death of the figure representing the social body that secures a transcendental form of continuity in the form of a patterned image.

Easily remembered because of its unique spatial and geometric form, such a patterned image connects generations, both living and dead. It is because such patterns grafted on to the body outlast, as images, the physical bodies of mortal men that they have come to fashion polities that define their existence in relation to ideas of immortality. Kinship and kingship in the Pacific are thus institutions of a body politic that thrives on ideals of eternity enshrined in pattern.

## Designing the Body

In designing the body, fibre and fabric are not just covering up or drawing attention but are subtly and occasionally overtly exerting influence. Hairstyle, jewelry of pigs' tusks, sharks' teeth and other accessories such as leaves, shells or even gold-plated teeth complement patterns worn on the body to create an overall look of vitality. Such patterns today come mostly in the form of the sarong, the most ubiquitous item of patterned clothing in the Pacific, known by locally specific names such as *lavalava* (Tonga), *laplap* (Papua New Guinea) or *sulu* (Fiji).

In the nineteenth century, garments and material substances of all kinds served to modify the outward appearance of Pacific Islanders' bodies, augmenting skins with the material qualities of artefacts. Wrappings, principally of fibre materials,

Preceding pages: Samoan tattooing designs covering waist, buttocks and thighs. Tattoos done by (from left to right) Petelo Suluape Su'a, Petelo Suluape Su'a and Alaiva'a Suluape Su'a, Auckland, New Zealand, 2004.

Opposite: Two young men wearing wrapped sarongs (*lavalava*), pigs' teeth and leaf decorations at the Teuila Festival, Apia, Samoa, 2003.

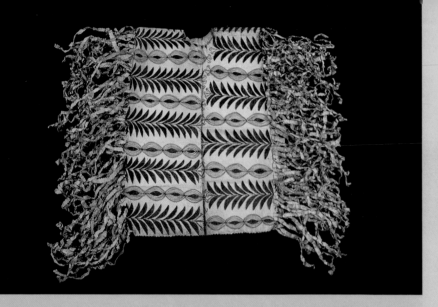

served to envelop the body in life and at death: patterned coverings, such as painted barkcloth wraps, finely woven pandanus mats, red feather helmets, leaf-fibre skirts and knotted coconut fibre tunics, as well as the indelible marks of tattoos, decorated the person. Layers of garments often denoted status, and geometric designs and motifs were visual indicators of the kinship ties of the wearer.

For instance, in eastern Polynesia elaborate feather cloaks and headdresses once signalled chiefly rank and alluded to divine presence, while in western Polynesia (e.g. Tonga and Samoa) finely woven pandanus mats tied around the waist were considered treasured possessions and were handed down through generations. In Tonga, fine mats such as *kie hingoa* (named mats) are still worn, wrapped around the waist, especially for important events such as royal visits and the King of Tonga's birthday celebrations.

In Tahiti, Niue and in the Cook Islands, nineteenth-century collections document the use of an upper-body garment known as a 'poncho'. Fashioned out of barkcloth, it was painted with freehand designs in Niue, while in the Cook Islands incisions

Above, left: Poncho, from Niue, made out of barkcloth with geometric patterns and fringe.

Above, right: Dancers from Tonga at the 8th Festival of Pacific Arts in Noumea, New Caledonia, 2000. The men on the left are wearing woven pandanus *ta'ovala* mats, while the two women are wearing *kiekie*, lattice-work girdles, around their waists.

Left: Barkcloth suit and headdress made to be worn at performances in the Cook Islands, *c.* 1900.

Opposite: Cook Island Poncho made of barkcloth, with cut-out patterns and coloured with turmeric.

were cut out of the fabric in a highly symmetrical fashion. As Christianity spread through Tahitian lay missionaries, the poncho became synonymous with high status and was adopted by chiefly ranks on other islands such as Samoa. Its former importance is still apparent in the Samoan two-piece dress known as *puletasi*, which is informing high fashion design there today.

Yet the decorative appeal of the art of the body as one of the lasting visual traits of the Pacific is only half the story. In order to have a fuller sense of the efficacy of patterns on the body, a detour into Pacific ideas of person and body is called for. The Western idea of the individual as a self-fashioning agent – as an independent being from birth – is alien to Pacific ideas which see the person as a divisible, corporeal and unstable entity, incorporating and divesting substances in a continuing process of transformation that permeates a person's life from birth to death. This transformation is normally done in sequence repeatedly throughout life, with a period of fasting and social separation being followed by an opening to the spirit world.

In life, across the Pacific, the body is not just unstable, it is also prone to dissipation and is subject to the perils of its metaphysical environment. These come from a dualistic world view, in which darkness, death and the gods have to be kept in balance with the world of the living. In Polynesia, but also commonly in Island Melanesia and Micronesia, the auspicious proximity of these realms is achieved through rendering activities, places and objects temporarily *tapu*, a condition of heightened sanctity that requires delicate management by priests or ritual experts. Desanctifying procedures such as washing or wrapping are at least as significant as sacrifices to the gods, as without them objects cannot return to ordinary life, but remain dangerous and potentially fatal as an uncontrolled life force.

In Polynesia, tattooing and wrapping the body in layers of fibre and fabric appear to have partially redressed this problematic permeability of the body. In Melanesia, on the other hand, more temporary measures, including paint and decorative accessories, are preferred. Whether in Polynesia or Melanesia, however, painted, printed or stamped geometric patterns and stylized motifs are used on a variety of body-covering media as well as other objects. In the Society Islands, for example, patterned designs on barkcloth ponchos also appeared as tattooing motifs.

Above, left: Hawaiian performers wearing headdresses, garlands and matching dresses during the 8th Festival of Pacific Arts, Noumea, New Caledonia, 2000.

Above, right: Tahitian performers wearing ponchos and leaf headdresses at the 7th Festival of Pacific Arts, Apia, Samoa, 1996. Performers from all over the Pacific converge at these highly popular gatherings which are generally filmed. Viewing performances on video tape is as popular as watching soap operas on television.

Below, right: Dancers from Tonga College performing at King Tupou IV's 85th birthday celebrations, Nuku'alofa, Tonga, 2003. King Tupou IV is the eldest son of the late Queen Salote, who gained notoriety for her promotion of traditional fibre arts in Tongan society.

Opposite, above, left: A group of female dancers from Lavengamalie College wear matching dresses and crowns to celebrate King Tupou IV's 85th birthday, Nuku'alofa, Tonga, 2003.

Spiral-shaped facial Maori tattoos can be found on carved, wooden feather boxes as well as on doorposts. In the Solomon Islands, curvilinear facial tattooing marks appear on carved, wooden canoe-prow figures, where the same curvilinear designs are incised in mother-of-pearl. This suggests that the human body was considered just as appropriate a 'canvas' for making visible patterned designs as barkcloth sheets and wooden carvings.

Easily the most prolific way of covering the body with removable patterns was through the production of barkcloth. Although no longer made in eastern Polynesia (e.g. Hawaii and the Cook Islands), barkcloth or *tapa* (as it is generically known in the Pacific) was manufactured across Polynesia, and it is still produced in Tonga and Fiji. Barkcloth was also manufactured across parts of Melanesia and, to a limited degree, in Micronesia. In New Britain, in Papua New Guinea, strips of dyed barkcloth would be wrapped around the waist as loincloths. Geometric and stylized designs painted on the strips represented local types of leaves, fruit and flowers. In Rennell and the Bellona Islands in the Solomons, barkcloth was dyed orange with turmeric root, which gives off a fragrant perfume, and was worn as a headband. On the island of Futuna, in Polynesia, strips of barkcloth known as *lafi* displayed intricate freehand, painted designs. These used to be worn as turbans and loincloths, but today have been transformed into part of the finery of a Futunan bride. Beautifully made dance aprons manufactured from thick barkcloth were worn in the Admiralty Islands, Papua New Guinea. Hanging from the cloth on threads were components such as shell beads, seeds and feathers, which were arranged in a grid so that they made a jangling sound as the dancer moved.

Barkcloth was not only a secondary layer of skin, it often also added a multi-sensory dimension to the essentially monochromatic tattooed skin, as the beaten bark was covered in perfumed paint substances whose coloration served as much to enhance the luminosity of the material as to strengthen the fabric through the varnishing effect of the pigment. As most barkcloth tears easily, is eaten by termites and wears out within a relatively short period of time, women's labour-intensive activities of stripping away the inner bark of the paper mulberry tree, soaking the strips, hammering them with a beater on an anvil and pasting sheets together to make larger cloth were continuous.

Above, right: Tahitian choir singing at the Heiva Festival in Papeete, Tahiti, French Polynesia, 1999. The guitar or string band, as it is known, has become an integral feature of contemporary Pacific performances.

Below, left: Niuean dancers at the 8th Festival of Pacific Arts, Noumea, New Caledonia, 2000. Performances in Polynesia and Melanesia involve arm, head, leg and feet movements that are choreographed to a musical accompaniment. Heavily orchestrated and regimented movements trace out patterns which tell a story with often genealogical and mythological importance, sung by an accompanying choir of men and women. Dress as well as jewelry emphasize the purposeful movements.

The sound of barkcloth being beaten still permeates villages in western Polynesia, where a solid wooden block is used as an anvil. In eastern Polynesia, the musical and rhythmic beating of the mallet was enhanced by a low, hollowed-out sounding board, supported on squat legs that were often carved. In some places, the percussion of the bark being beaten was seen as transmitting messages, as in Hawaii, where the legendary character Kamoeau was said to learn everything about a woman by hearing her beating. The soundscape of barkcloth, in fact, evokes that of tattooing, which like the beating of the bark is accompanied by

Opposite and above: Bodies were transformed through decoration throughout the Pacific and acted as a means to make visible social, political and religious affiliations. From left to right: Highlands man from Papua New Guinea with face paint, shell body decorations and feathers, 7th Festival of Pacific Arts, Apia, Samoa, 1996; Highlands man from Papua New Guinea with feather

headdress, wig, bead decoration and face paint, 7th Festival of Pacific Arts, Apia, Samoa, 1996; High Chief of Samoa wearing an elaborate crown with necklace of pigs' tusks, c. 1910.

Overleaf: A Highlands man from Papua New Guinea makes final preparations for a dance at the 7th Festival of Pacific Arts, Apia, Samoa, 1996.

songs when it is tapped into the skin. In this way, while profoundly visual in their effect, the designs on both body and fibre allude to a conceptual aspect of pattern that eludes the eye.

Even though wrappings, body decoration and tattooing appear to be quite separate, they are all centred on the social design of the body. Wrapping is about dressing the body; body painting is the temporary application of paint to the surface of the skin; and tattooing involves marking the skin with indelible designs through a combination of (sometimes incidental) blood-letting and subcutaneous depositing of pigment. Scarification is distinct from tattooing in that it does not have to involve pigmentation. The simplistic assumption that these processes of self-presentation centre on separate aesthetic sensibilities understates their importance.

All over the Pacific people ornament themselves for important occasions, and this self-decoration is something more than a matter of fashion and cosmetics. The decoration of the body is a medium through which people demonstrate their relationships to ancestral spirits, express certain ideals and emotions, and make statements about social and religious values. In many cases decorations are themselves valuables, transmitted through exchanges; other items, such as feathers and shells, must be obtained through trade or hunting.

Dances are the most important occasions for the donning of body decorations. They are almost always competitive events at which a desire for health, strength, fertility and prosperity is expressed. In the Highlands of Papua New Guinea, outbreaks of inter-tribal warfare oscillate with exchanges and dancing displays, at which dancers seek both to attract future alliances and to demonstrate allegiance in the present.

In Mount Hagen, in the central plateau of Papua New Guinea, self-decoration is the antithesis of mourning. While in mourning the body is neglected, dirtied, darkened with charcoal or even mutilated by tearing out hair, in times of prosperity material success and physical health are thought to be visible in a bodily condition that is enlarged through the wearing of headdresses and is made to shine and gleam in the sun through the application of oil on the skin. Magical qualities are ascribed to certain elaborate decorations such as the *kilt* wig, which is made from a bright-flowering tree that is known to attract birds (in the same way that men hope to attract women), or the 'pig's tail'

apron, which imparts to the wearer an appearance judged to be as prestigious as the 'white fat' of the pigs they represent. Wearing red ochre is thought to increase one's attractiveness across Melanesia, where girls, pigs and valuables are said to 'follow' the ochre's fragrant smell; oil and grease are also used as commonplace enhancements, as they give the skin a healthy glow and heighten strength and sexual attractiveness.

When an item of decoration is worn, a connection is made between the idealized attributes of the article and the person wearing it, so much so that the wearer is taken to demonstrate the efficacy of the item. In Mount Hagen, the feathers of certain birds – such as the Sicklebill, the Princess Stephanie, the White Bird of Paradise and red parrots – and the skin of numerous kinds of marsupials are sought-after ornaments. Wearing red bird-plumes associates the dancer with the graceful movements of this Bird of Paradise when it displays itself before females; while use of the eagle feather draws comparisons between a bird of prey and a wealth-seeking man. Certain shells are desired because of their shiny quality. In the past, when shells were scarcer, bright pearl shells in particular were withdrawn from circulation and hidden inside the owner's men's house, for it was thought that their gleam would attract other shells to them and make the owner successful in competitive exchanges.

Portable items of decoration may drastically alter the perception of a person's body. As an additional (and removable) layer to the body's surface, such decorations – whether shells, barkcloth or feathers – highlight the skin's dual role as a protective shield and a permeable membrane (exuding liquids and odour) and provoke associations with certain living things, including plants and trees. We may want to think about what people put on their skin in the same way that we view food – that is, as a substance which is capable of transforming the appearance of a person, and with it the social effect of that person. Here we discuss three types of substances that are used in different parts of the Pacific to transform the appearance of the skin: hair, paint and the indelible mark (tattooing).

## Hair

The ambiguity of a concept of body that centres on its skin is highlighted with hair, an inner, hard and bone-like substance of

the body that surfaces on the outside, where it appears as a soft and permeable cover. As something that transgresses the physical boundary of the body, hair is an object of attention the world over. In the Pacific, the cutting of hair to signal the end of mourning, or the onset of adult life in men, is usually marked by a ceremony. In the Cook Islands of eastern Polynesia, boys whose hair has been left to grow since birth are made to sit upon specially made quilts. Close relatives each take a lock of hair, and in this way symbolically welcome the young man into society. It is through such acts of transforming hair from a bodily substance into an

artefact, allowing locks of hair to become analogous with cordage, that salient concepts of personhood are objectified and become the basis for value judgments and social distinction.

Particularly elaborate feather headdresses or wigs are used to cover hair in the central Highlands of Papua New Guinea and in the markedly stratified societies of Hawaii and the Society Islands, but were produced, to some degree, everywhere in Polynesia. In the Highlands of Papua New Guinea, where competitive exchanges called *moka* decide prestige and influence over others, wearing plumes of different bird species indicates the onset,

Preceding pages, left: 'A Samoan village Belle in festive dress', late nineteenth century.

Preceding pages, right: A man with bound head and small net bag around his neck, New Guinea, c. 1900.

Opposite: Rapanui (Easter Island) performer at the 8th Festival of Pacific Arts, Noumea, New Caledonia, 2000.

Above: Rapanui dancer at the 8th Festival of Pacific Arts, Noumea, New Caledonia, 2000.

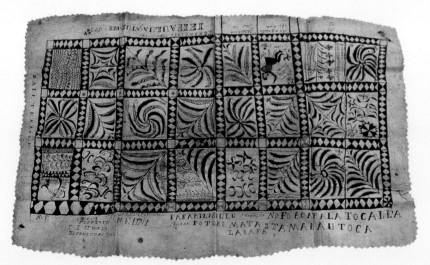

climax and ending of the cycle of exchanges; while heavy wigs – lined with scarab beetles and marsupial furs, and brightly painted with a variety of designs – are worn by certain men obeying strict taboos during the festivities. Wigs are distinguished according to their length. Some consist of elaborate structures made of cane strips, bound with lianas to which lengths of hair are fastened, and lumps of heated resin from a tree whose red flowers are noted for attracting flocks of birds. Others are more like hair-settings: the growing hair of the men themselves is teased into a dome, rope is woven into it to make it stiff, and tree oil and resin are kneaded straight in. Different versions of wigs can be worn on a rather wide range of occasions. As wig-wearing demands taboo-abiding men, who are at the peak of their health and aggression, to conserve their strength, the wig reveals some of the ambiguities of a status symbol whose capacity to attract carries its own risks by exposing the wearer to the potentially harmful effects of sorcery.

Hair and its complement, the feather, figured prominently in the artefacts of rank across Micronesia and the eastern Pacific. Most notable were the fly whisks of the Austral Islands and the Society Islands, as well as feather capes and girdles from the Hawaiian and Society Islands. Some of these objects were only broadly associated with status, while others were more directly linked with chiefly titles: to wear the girdle was to possess the title.

In Polynesia, feathers generally conveyed sacredness and were intimately connected with the gods. Any feather artefact enhanced the efficacy and divinity of its wearer, and long feather sashes and girdles worn in the Society Islands were even associated with particular gods and former title-holders. The feather object, as well as being a substance charged with divine presence, was a material genealogy that connected, by its presence, both divine ancestors and previous rulers with a living individual.

In the Cook Islands, sashes were also chiefly regalia but were made of plaited pandanus (rather than flax and feathers used in the Hawaiian Islands). This points to the connection of women's cloth and plait-work artforms with sovereignty and sacredness, and there is plenty of other evidence for this. This does not mean, however, that we should conclude that there were male and female forms of regalia, as the important element of Polynesian chieftainship was not the gender of generative power but the maintenance of a genealogical link with ancestral deities, who ensured growth and life. Patterned artefacts, whether covered in feathers or consisting of plaited patterns, were manifestations of such a link – as were agricultural fertility, rich fishing harvests and good health – condensing the remembrances of times past into a single moment.

## Paint

One of the most important substances used to strike a likeness that draws out the potential of the decorated skin is paint, which appears as colour (although it is not its equal). Paint, as substance, not only has visual qualities of sheen and hue, but it also has smell and even sound qualities (associated with the pitch of colour terms when uttered).

The aural associations of paint are particularly important in areas of dense forestation, where sight does not travel far and the dead are believed to reside on the perimeter of the world of the living, above the treetops, and to communicate through the voices of the birds. While the sound of paint, like the uttering

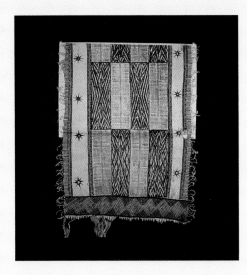

Opposite, left: Barkcloth from Niue with naturalistic motifs drawn in a grid-like formation by hand.

Opposite, right: Detail of Samoan barkcloth, Apia, Samoa, 2003.

Above: Strip of barkcloth, called *masi*, worn as a loin cloth from Fiji, early nineteenth century. Patterns were produced by a combination of freehand painting, cut-out stencils and rubbing over patterned block with pigment.

Right: Dancer from Papua New Guinea, 7th Festival of the Pacific Arts, Apia, Samoa, 1996.

Overleaf, left: Patterned wooden paddle from the Austral Islands. The technique of carving regular geometric shapes into wood is reminiscent of tattooing patterns.

of a spell, can change the experience of the skin, its smells allude to a world beyond. The choice of paint substances with regard to their smell is particularly prominent in island regions, where the dead are believed to reside beyond the horizon, in a world parallel to, yet distanced from, the living. Certain island regions of Melanesia are notorious for the strong odour of the paints used, which even today are preferred to shop-bought paints.

The most widely distributed colouring material in the Pacific is turmeric, a source of yellow shades ranging from rich cream to deep orange. Infusions of the grated root of this plant, which are aromatic, are used as dye and are applied to barkcloth. Turmeric-dyed barkcloth is commonly reserved for persons of rank to mark childbirth, marriages, initiations, mourning and death. Another source for yellow is the blossom of a citrus tree, which in Melanesia is preferred because of the medicinal effect ascribed to its aroma.

Eastern Polynesia is famous for its brilliant reds, especially that of nineteenth-century barkcloth from the Society Islands, which is derived from a combination of juices from berries and leaves. On most of the barkcloth-making islands brown and black dyes are made from the candle-nut, whose inner bark can be used as a dye or a kind of surface glaze. Black from the soot of burnt candle-nuts is used in tattooing as well as in barkcloth-making. Resinous brown saps from ironwood, or from a species of mangrove, are used as adhesive to bind sheets of barkcloth together and as a kind of varnish that makes barkcloth waterproof.

Earthen pigments are another major source of paint substances. In western Polynesia and Melanesia, red clays are carefully processed into blocks, grated and applied by women to barkcloth, using one of the brown saps as a fixative. In Fiji, there are people whose job it is to extract clay from a valued deposit, while dangerous journeys are undertaken on Papua New Guinea's Sepik River to obtain renowned clay. Perhaps the most elaborate use of ochre is to be found among the Elema people of the Papuan Gulf, who used to colour the elaborate masks of a ceremonial cycle with splendid pink and red ochre, yellow clay and grey soapstone, in addition to charcoal and burnt lime.

The uses of particular plants, trees or earthen pigments are highly specific. They are valued because of the material analogies they suggest, rather than because of the symbolic significance of the resulting colour. Burnt lime, for example, is significant across Melanesia for the marking of patterns that are ancestrally sanctioned or charged. Lime is taken from the bottom of an earth-oven, deposited there as residue of the frequent heating of stones or, alternatively, from dried coral from the sea. Lime is thus likened to ancestral forces associated with the remains of acts of renewal.

## The Indelible Mark

Whenever a paint substance is applied, whether directly on the skin or on one of its membrane-like substitutes, it is embedded in a linear outline that is drawn, rubbed or carved. Barkcloth patterns, as well as the indelible mark of the tattoo, are applied with a range of instruments, from printing stamps to brushes made from pandanus fruit or coconut husks. Stamps as well as stencils secure the even repetition of the design across large areas, as does the method of rubbing sheets of beaten bark over boards carved with designs. While the paint substance quickly becomes brittle, fades or washes off, the lines remain visible long after.

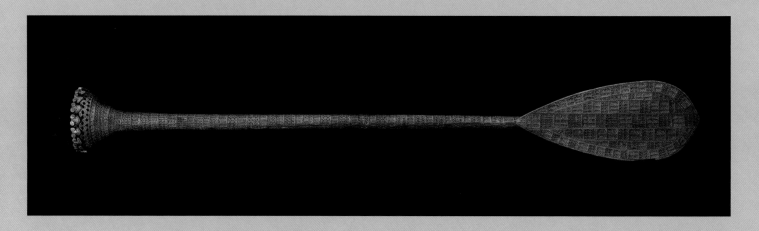

Left: Eighteenth-century Maori feather box featuring curvilinear designs that also appear in Maori tattooing. Such boxes were used to store personal ornaments and valuables.

Below: Tattooed girls with shell and dogs' teeth decorations, Central Province, Papua New Guinea, c. 1900.

Left: Samoan tattooist Tulouena Maleko Palea uses a pig's tusk to produce traditional tattoos, Auckland, New Zealand, 2004.

Opposite: Inia Taylor uses modern tattooing tools to create contemporary Maori tattooing designs, Grey Lynn, Auckland, New Zealand, 2004.

Densely and repetitively applied lines disrupt the perception of the viewer, presenting a visually distracting, disorientating and unstable multiplication of structure. Nowhere else is this quality more exploited than in tattooing, which was widely practised in the eastern Pacific. The word tattoo derives from Polynesian languages, and the original term, *tatau*, is still used in Samoa and Tahiti. Missionaries in the Marquesas Islands reported the custom of whole body tattooing among warriors, using densely packed geometric motifs.

Tattoos of fine lines and curvilinear forms based on areas of alternating contrast bear a remarkable likeness to the carved geometric incisions on the surfaces of paddles, feather boxes, shields and shell valuables as well as other artefacts. This striking resemblance between patterns marked on the skin and those carved into wood or shell highlights the life-giving qualities that are associated with bodies and materials as indexes of life, light and growth. The intricately carved paddle of the Austral Islands (see page 158) embodies similar ideas. The paddle, like the whole body tattoo, may appear as an effective recomposition of the body, rendering it inviolable to sacred forces emanating from the sea. However, it also exhibits the profoundly ambiguous character of pattern – its protective role but also its acknowledgment of mortality.

The Marquesan practice of removing skin on death is the prime example. While a whole body tattoo (like a shield in battle) served to insulate and deconsecrate a warrior, providing protection through the disorientating effect of the patterned skin, this was never more than a temporary measure; for the need for such protection acknowledges the inherent vulnerability of the tattooed person, whose mortality is reconciled with the fact that the tattooed skin is the ultimate gift to the gods at death.

The importance of removing patterns for the restoration of sanctity is consistent with the fact that certain individuals who were chiefs of the highest rank were not tattooed. Tattooing had to be removed in order to recover the absolute disembodied sacredness that characterizes immortality in the world. It is for the same reason that, in Melanesia, patterning the body with paint substances and decorations was stressed as a temporary phase in a person's life that coincided with moments of heightened vulnerability, such as in initiation, marriage and death.

It is thus no coincidence, given the difficulty of removing tattoos, that patterning the body with lines generally utilized more ephemeral means, or was tempered by the use of secondary skins working as wraps. Creating a visually disorientating density and destabilizing effect similar to whole body tattooing was made possible by using *kupesi* (design boards).

Above: Tattooing design by the
Tahitian tattooist Ra'a Poto,
Auckland, New Zealand, 2004.

Right: A Hawaiian performer
with geometric tattoos, shell
necklace and leaf headdress,
8th Festival of the Pacific Arts,
Noumea, New Caledonia, 2000.

Opposite: Detail of a tattooing
design by the Tahitian tattooist
Ra'a Poto, Auckland, New
Zealand, 2004.

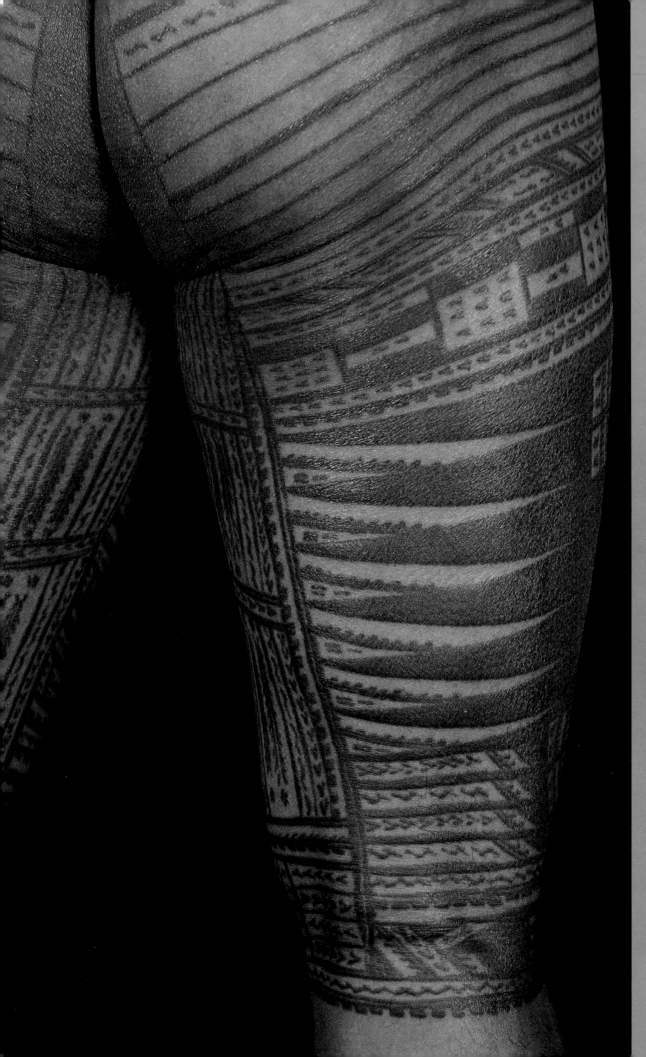

Left: Tattoos by the artist Alaiva'a Suluape Su'a, New Zealand, 2004.

Opposite: Detail of traditional Maori tattoo by Derek Lardelli, Auckland, New Zealand, 2004. The tattoo design is called 'Puhoro'.

Overleaf, left: In the twentieth century, tattooing and material substances of all kinds served to modify the outward appearance of Pacific islanders' bodies. In the Sepik region of Papua New Guinea, this process still holds today: skin is sliced with a bamboo sliver as part of an initiation ceremony to produce scars that resemble the teeth of the crocodile.

Overleaf, right: Solomon Islands shield with figure of mother-of-pearl inlay, mid-nineteenth century. It is made from plaited cane overlaid with putty nut and inset with shell. Such shields were commonly used in warfare, and as items of wealth, they were probably obtained through exchange and carried as a sign of prestige.

Pages 168–169: Solomon Island dancer with facial scarification, 7th Festival of the Pacific Arts, Apia, Samoa, 1996. Scarification is a means of permanently marking the skin by cutting alone, without the use of pigments. As a form of self-violence, it is often associated with rites of passage marking the stages that lead from adolescence into adult life.

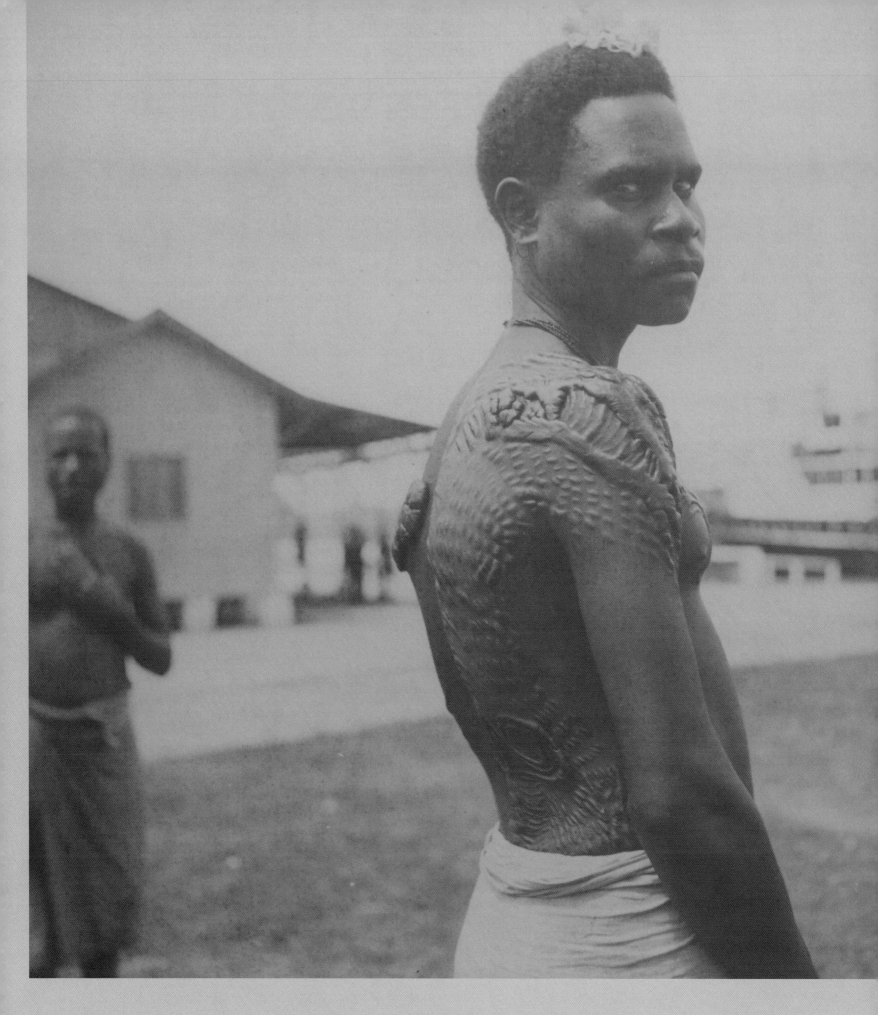

*Kupeti* (the Samoan spelling of *kupesi*) are still used in Samoa for the production of *siapo* (sheets of barkcloth). It has been suggested that barkcloth-making continued to be practised in western Polynesia because of the methods of manufacture used there, which, instead of involving laborious felting, used resin saps to glue sheets of beaten bark together. As the cloth is often decorated with repeated patterns created by rubbing dye into the fabric at the same time as individual strips are being pasted together on the design tablets, a completed barkcloth may reveal many different repeated patterns, each metaphorically referring to distinct parts of a family, or the distinctly patterned parts of a tattooed body.

In the past design boards consisted of a double layer of strong, smooth strips of pandanus leaf, stitched together. The raised design patterns were built up on the upper surface of the pandanus base by sewing thin sticks of split bamboo, strips of folded pandanus leaf or sinnet cord on to it. Visual sources for the designs were everyday things, such as rolled pandanus leaves or flowers, sinnet cordage, shells, banana pods or the midribs of the coconut palm leaves made into brushes or brooms. A number of these design tablets were arranged and fastened down on a curved section of an old canoe hull, called the *papa*, upon which strips of barkcloth were assembled and sometimes even drawn freehand. Carved, wooden boards have today replaced these leafy design boards, as much of the manufacture of barkcloth is for the commercial market and is rather small in size. For truly large pieces of barkcloth, Samoans today turn to the Tongans, who are still producing huge lengths. In Tonga, the making of wooden design boards used to be the prerogative of women of high rank, who are still expected to preside over the women's organizations responsible for the production of barkcloth.

Design boards are no longer used in Fiji, where stencils now predominate; while in Futuna hand-painted criss-cross designs and finely ruled lines appear to translate the distinctive patterns of the much admired plaited mats of the Marshall Islanders to the north. Such variation in patterning techniques suggests that we should look at pattern not as a product, but as a process that is interpreted in a number of ways – as a performance, as an attractive cover or as a protective shield that serves to desanctify temporarily whatever it covers.

Although modern innovations are carved into driftwood, the design boards, like the coconut leaf *kupeti*, remind us of the nature of pattern. The materials – coconut and driftwood – suggest an association with movement and displacement, as they drift from island to island washing ashore. Like the coconut and driftwood, people too have migrated across the Pacific, and still do so, whether on trade journeys or visits to natal villages or urban centres. Putting down new roots far from home, people are reminded of connections by the patterns that cover the surfaces of their bodies.

These patterns are not simply reflections upon the past but, like the coconut and driftwood, their presence guarantees a pathway into the future. Patterns on the house and the body capture ways of life that we take for granted and ideas about future prosperity. The ability of patterns to transplant themselves across generations and regions turns them into unique carriers of ideas about the world, which in time come to seem as real as the products in which they are embedded. The question that this now raises is exactly how pattern comes to be a thing of the mind.

167

PATTERNS
OF THE
MIND

6

Preceding pages: Detail of 1960s *tivaivai 'taorei'*, Rarotonga, Cook Islands, 2003. Patchwork patterns such as these are remembered in terms of units of coloured sequences of numbers, enabling women to construct large identical areas of matching patterns based on the same sequence.

Above, right: Soul catcher made of coconut fibre from Pukapuka, Cook Islands, 1876.

Below: Illustration of the soul-trap in use in the Reverend William Wyatt Gill's *Life in Southern Isles*, 1876 (page 181). According to Gill's interpretation, when a person was ill, a soul catcher was suspended from a tree and any bird or insect flying into one of the loops would be believed to be the soul of the ailing person. The trapped soul could thereby be recovered by making offerings to local priests.

Opposite: Marshall Island navigation chart made from cane sticks, fibre and shells. These charts were prototypical models of swell and wave patterns in the waters around the coral atolls of eastern Micronesia. Small shells incorporated into the chart represented the position of islands, though, generally, the charts acted as a mnemonic device, as they were not carried on sea voyages.

Patterning, far from being a neutral or unremarkable artistic activity, has effects much more enduring than the often ephemeral media that serve as its vehicle, because it casts ideas about who we are into highly communicable forms. These forms – whether curvilinear incisions, diagonally plaited leaf fronds or products of a rhythmic movement of a line along a plane – give rise to the opportunity of limitless innovation beyond the specific boundaries of a particular culture. Patterning, as a repetitive, rhythmic and highly ordered activity, is thus able to act as a building-block in putting new ideas into practice, a fact we appreciate when we say that patterns are 'good to think with'.

Indeed, pattern – the symmetrical transformation of a unit motif along a surface, with its appealing logical quality and its schematic, rhythmic, gestural and highly standardized form – both attracts and resists memory. As the anthropologist Alfred Gell has suggested, pattern serves as a 'mind trap' that entrances perception in an often time-consuming effort to fathom out how it came into being. Pattern, in the first instance, may appear the most tangible of entities, yet it can only be articulated in our mind. As a thing of the mind, it is uniquely portable and translatable across different media. Pattern's longevity and global resonance contribute to its role as a 'leitmotif' of design capable of mapping the future.

Pattern alone is able to address a question that is unique to the Pacific. With three quarters of the population in the Pacific Islands living in the urban centres of Australia, New Zealand, North America and Europe, a Pacific identity that articulates presence and absence has to be fashioned – when one is far away from home, securing and consolidating connections becomes a matter of urgency. Pattern ideally bridges these spatial divides, as its bodily (gestural) and mental (memorable) portability offers the opportunity for diaspora communities to trace and transmit genealogical connections. In performance, patterns often appear, subtly, as open-ended likenesses or as devices that fashion recognition of the meaning of belonging. This has famously been

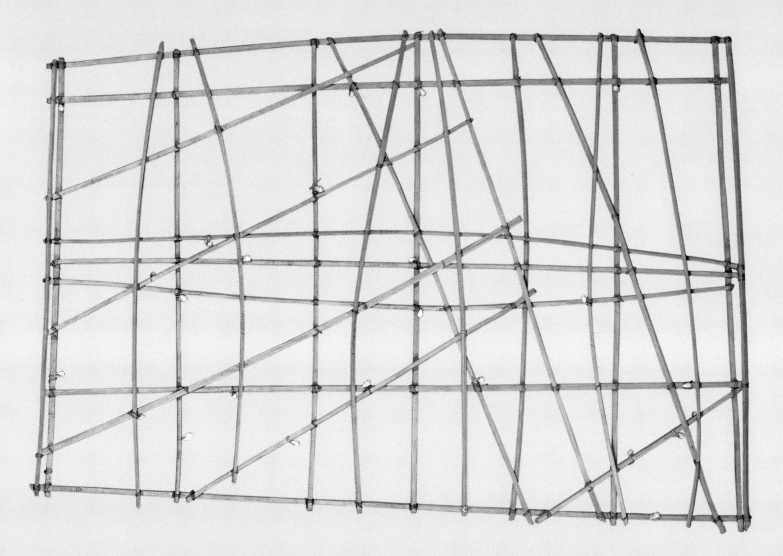

argued by the anthropologist and curator Adrienne Kaeppler, who describes how rhythmic movements in Tongan dance are played out in barkcloth designs, kinship relations and poetry.

While pattern is conservative, in as much as it functions through repetition, it is also a key aspect of innovation. Its reproduction will be more convincing when executed by the mind and tempered by its inevitable transformation. Abstract and, frequently, unspecific in nature, pattern is akin to a 'burial place of memory', where all pasts are equally present and where to recall means to transform. This is similar to the way in which classical poetry utilized the theme of the underworld to issue forth ever new, and yet instantly recognizable, versions of events that made history by being retold over and over again.

These ideas are tangible in the so-called 'stick charts' from the Marshall Islands which were used as both prototypical teaching tools as well as actual representations of sea movements around island archipelagos. As external mnemonic devices, the grid-like pattern enabled the internalization of navigational knowledge, thus equipping Micronesian seafarers to undertake long-distance voyaging safely across open sea. Likewise the looped and knotted 'soul catcher' made from cordage in Pukapuka, one of the northern atolls of the Cook Islands, was supposedly woven to capture the drifting souls of those afflicted with illness which were transformed into either a bird or insect.

Pattern in the Pacific has continued to be asserted as the hallmark of modernity and of future-orientated fashion. Fibre and pattern in the Pacific work to the same end, as they unravel our normative topological understanding of the spatial nature of the surfaces of objects. In emphasizing transformation, patterned fibre and fabric force us to consider the topology of objects from a temporal perspective. This interplay of temporal and spatial dimensions in the topology of objects is most evident in string figures, which, as much as they are playful pastimes, bring to mind genealogical connections that help resolve relations in social and political life.

GIRLS MAKING TAPA NUKUALOFA

Two examples illustrate the continuing relevance of topological thinking in the innovative use of fibre-like materials in the Pacific. The first explores the patterns in openwork designs in Tongan fibre arts. Drawing on a range of intricate woven and string-based designs – both in historical and contemporary contexts – we trace out the spatial, temporal and cosmological ideas invoked there by lattice-work and cordage.

The second case-study takes up the contemporary use of floral imagery in the Pacific as something that is not just, as one might assume, for visual pleasure. In fact, the use of flowers provokes associations ranging from the olfactory to the spatial and situational. This study of Cook Island *tivaivai* will illustrate the interplay of floral imagery with cultural memory and techniques of recollection. A focus on the patchwork quilt technique will further explore the relation between coloured quilting patterns, topological ideas and memory.

## String and Square in Tonga

Tongan society was, to a large extent, based on fibre technology. Coir threads, several species of pandanus and coconut palm leaves, and the bark of paper mulberry and breadfruit trees were among the many fibrous materials utilized by Tongan women to make baskets, aprons, mats and wrappings of all sorts. Captain James Cook's collection of fibre arts is testament to the remarkable breadth of design of the fibre-based products there, and provides us with an insight into the extraordinary vision of the Tongan women who invested so much in these natural materials. Even with the mass importation of European fabrics and fashions, Tongan fibre arts have maintained their significance in ritual and everyday life to this day. Not only do aprons, mats,

girdles and barkcloth denote an external form of Tongan identity, but their ostentatious display at life-cycle events also reflects a sense of the wearer's social position within a society deeply concerned with hierarchy.

Pre-constitutional Tonga adhered to a rigid hierarchical system based on status and rank that still continues today. A series of myths explain the social divisions between the ruling elite and the common people. According to these, the god Tangaloa came down from the sky on a tree and lived with a mortal woman, a descendant of a worm who inhabited the earth. She gave birth to their child, 'Aho'eitu, who became the first Tongan chief, the Tu'i Tonga, the divine ancestor of all Tongans of high rank. Commoners (*tu'a*), in contrast, are considered to be descendants of the worm. Tongan chiefs claim to be related to this first Tongan chief, 'Aho'eitu, the level of chiefly rank being a factor of their line of descent from the Tu'i Tonga.

Fibre products worn by Tongans reflect rank and status. Certain types of barkcloth and mat are categorized by Tongans as *koloa*, a term used to describe objects of considerable wealth. *Koloa* can be presented, exchanged or worn on special occasions such as births, deaths, marriages and initiation ceremonies. *Koloa* takes its most valuable form in woven pandanus mats (*ta'ovala*), which are as smooth as silk and fringed with red parrot feathers, and are wrapped around the waist of the ruling elite at special occasions or presented to someone of chiefly rank. Of slightly lesser value are single lengths of barkcloth (*ngatu*), which are sometimes as much as one hundred metres long. These denote the importance of the wearer or, if gifted, are intended to impress the recipient.

Other patterned fibre valuables also rely on visual openwork designs that draw attention to the product as well as the wearer. Some of the most eye-catching pieces exhibiting these openwork designs are intricately woven lattice-work aprons, threaded from the fibres of coconut husks and decorated with polished shells and beads. Detailed attention is even paid to the design of baskets: in Cook's collection we find oval baskets constructed from alternating coloured geometric shapes surrounded by a luminous ring of tiny white shells. Such baskets – made from woven coconut fibres – were reserved for use by chiefly women, who carried strips of perfumed barkcloth inside them. Their visual effect relies, in part, on the alignment of alternating triangles of brown and black, and is further accentuated by a neatly arranged fine white line of shiny shells. The resulting openwork patterns – running in both horizontal and vertical directions – appear as a lattice-work design based on a grid of squares.

Adrienne Kaeppler argues that openwork designs – what she calls the decorative element (*teuteu*) of Tongan fibre arts – enhance the effects of *koloa*, forming one of three interrelated bases of Tongan design. These ordering principles follow the same structure as Tongan music, with its key components of melody (*fasi*), drone (*laulalo*) and decoration (*teuteu*). Furthermore, Kaeppler adds, these three-part structural relations are played out in Tongan dance performances, poetry and social structures as well as in the production and decoration of fibre-based arts. The deep-rootedness of this logic, Kaeppler argues, means that the lattice-work designs – the grid of regular squares that appears on the surface of barkcloth, woven aprons and other

*koloa* – can be understood as a visual expression of the hierarchical nature of Tongan society.

Despite the underlying structure Kaeppler attributes to Tongan fibre arts, the material qualities of lattice-work vegetable fibres should not be overlooked. Their resemblance to baskets is critical to an understanding of Tongan design and its significance. As lattice-work designs take on the form of basketry, ideas of containment inherent to the material nature of lattice-work make them effective as stable reference points for genealogy, representing not only chiefly relationships to the gods, but also the connecting forces binding all other social relations in Tonga. Moreover, lattice-work designs both bring to the fore ideas of containment because of their visual resemblance to basketry and because of the physical engagement of the body in their production. Fibre threads – whether twisted, beaten, whittled, stretched or knotted – thus carry forward ideas that find material expression in lengths of barkcloth, woven aprons, string figures or crocheted overskirts worn around the waist, as we now show.

## Barkcloth

Barkcloth (*ngatu*) continues to be manufactured in Tonga. The environment on the Tongan island of Tongatapu is particularly suited to the cultivation of the paper mulberry tree, and it is here that most barkcloth is produced.

Opposite, left: Barkcloth-making in Nuku'alofa, Tonga.

Opposite, right: *Kupesi* barkcloth design stencil from Tonga, 1994. It was made from a plaited pandanus palm leaf and coconut spathe base, with pattern of coconut ribs wrapped with strands of coconut husk, fastened to base with hibiscus bast.

Right: Losana Amore paints barkcloth designs in Mua, Tongatapu, Tonga, 2003.

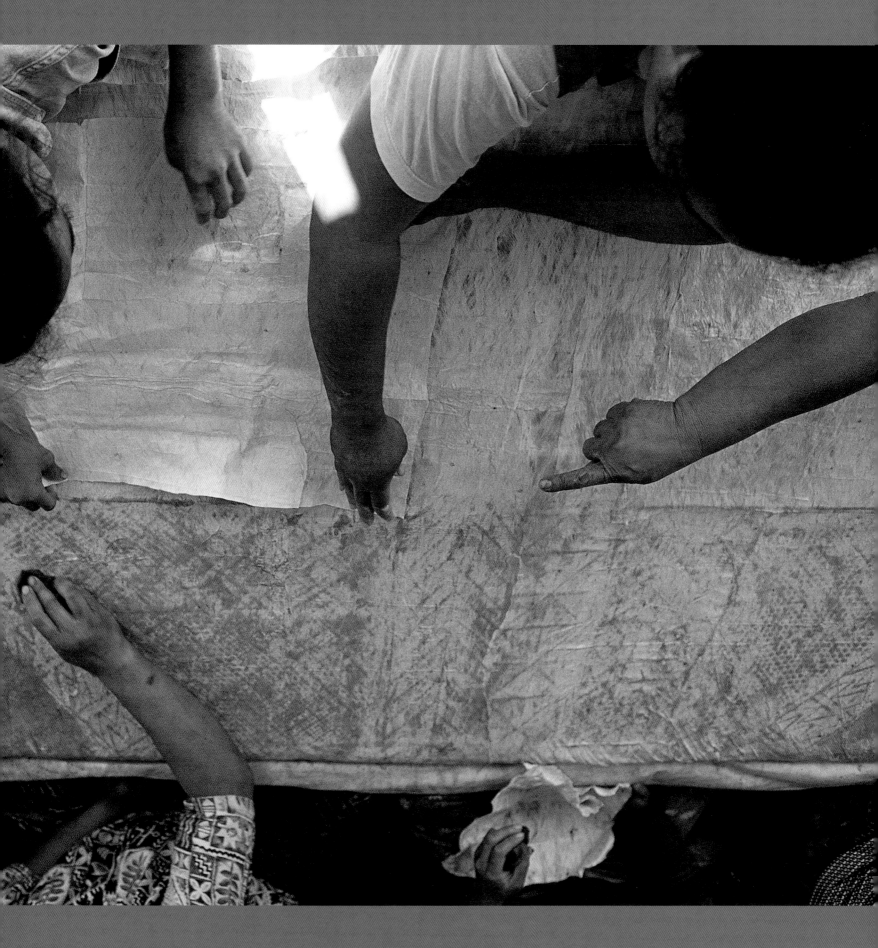

Here, as elsewhere in the Pacific, barkcloth production is controlled principally by women; in pre-constitutional Tonga it was chiefly women who sanctioned its production and reserved the right to apply patterns to the surface in the final stages of completion.

After stripping the inner bark of the paper mulberry, women soak the bark in water before they scrape it to smooth its surface. The bast is then beaten on a wooden anvil (*tutua*) with a wooden mallet (*ike*) that has two grooved sides for widening the bark and two smooth sides for finishing it. Pairs of strips of bark are overlapped, moistened, and then hit repeatedly, producing the rhythmic beat that sounds out across the island. The result is a strip of barkcloth, known as a *feta'aki*, with a considerably enlarged surface area.

Piles of *feta'aki* remain stored in houses until women require them to produce sheets of barkcloth. When ready, women assemble in special groups to produce lengths of barkcloth, gathering round a convex table (*papa koko'anga*) on top of which wooden rubbing blocks and a grid of coconut leaflets sewn together into a special design are placed. Sitting in pairs, facing each other, the women place rolls of *feta'aki* over the table, pasting together the overlapping edges with a brown resin made from arrowroot tubers. Large sheets of barkcloth are made by joining together two layers of *feta'aki*, back to back. Additional *feta'aki* are added, each at right angles to the last, then rubbed with the resin to leave the raised *kupesi* design imprinted on its outstretched surface. The process of joining strips of barkcloth and rubbing dyes on to the surface continues until the barkcloth reaches its required length.

As each section of the barkcloth is passed down the row of women sitting around the bench, the total number of completed units is counted. The length of barkcloth is recorded in units called *langanga*, which correspond to half the length of the rubbing bench – typically between 1 and 2 feet (0.3 to 0.6 metres). An entire barkcloth may extend beyond fifty *langanga* in length.

This unit of measurement sometimes appears as hand-painted dividing lines and numbers painted on the surface of the barkcloth. Women may also apply additional motifs – such as geometric shapes, abstract patterns and naturalistic images – painted with black or brown paints. Some barkcloth designs feature images of historical events, such as the sighting of Halley's Comet over Tonga in 1910, or the funding of RAF fighter aircraft by Tongans during the Second World War.

Page 176: *Kupesi* design stencils arranged on barkcloth ready for printing, Mua, Tongatapu, Tonga, 2003.

Page 177: Rubbing *kupesi* design stencils to create patterns, Mua, Tongatapu, Tonga, 2003.

Preceding pages: Painting barkcloth designs, Mua, Tongatapu, Tonga, 2003. From left to right: Uini Moala, Lavelua Nusi, Losana Mone and Alisi Kanonga Ta'a. Lengths of barkcloth gifted during life-cycle events are indicative of the influence and prestige a receiving family wields in Tongan society. Giving barkcloth also bestows prestige on the giver.

Above: Tongan lattice-work girdle, *sisi fale*, collected during Captain James Cook's voyages during the late eighteenth century. Such girdles are no longer worn in Tongan society but have been replaced by a new form of girdle, *kiekie*, worn by women, which is based on a similar openwork design.

Opposite: String figure from the Torres Straits Islands. String figures such as these were constructed all over the Pacific. Not only did they provide entertainment and pass the time, but these figures were also used to transmit cosmological and astrological knowledge.

The delicate lattice-work designs generated by the *kupesi* (tied together with coir fibres and rubbed on to the surface of the barkcloth) act as visual reference points for Tongans recalling genealogies of chiefly connections to divine ancestors, as the *kupesi* are passed down through chiefly lineages. Furthermore, it is the length of the patterns and the incorporation of a great many (though finite) number of strips of *feta'aki*, measured in *langanga*, that connote the social standing of the intended recipient and also the connecting force between the kinship relations who have invested in the production of the cloth. It is the material and technical engagement of women in the production of barkcloth – the pooling of corporate material resources and the execution of technical knowledge in transforming a natural fibre into *koloa* – that allows kinship connections and social memory to be tied into the display of whole pieces of barkcloth.

## Woven Aprons (*Sisi Fale*)

The *sisi fale* is an intricate brown apron of intertwined coconut fibres woven into a lattice-work design, almost like a basket. Attached to its grid-like structure are a number of woven rings (also of coconut fibre), strips of plaited fibre and a number of shell beads, animal teeth, carved pieces of whale ivory and small red feathers. Although they were discontinued when Tonga passed into constitutional rule, Adrienne Kaeppler notes that at the time of Captain James Cook's visits to Tonga these were considered to be high-ranking aprons, and were primarily worn by the Tu'i Tonga, his sister and his sister's daughter, as well as other descendants of the chiefly line. Red feathers, coconut fibre and whale ivory were particularly befitting for chiefly nobles, as in Polynesia these materials were considered highly sacred.

Cook made the observation that, 'They have also a curious apron, made of the out side fibres of the Cocoanut shell and composed of a number of small pieces sewed together in such a manner as to form stars, half Moons, little squars, etc., and studed with beads of shells and covered with red feathers, so as to have a pretty effect.' Indeed, it is reasonable to propose that the arrangement of valuable materials into the form of stars and moons implies an association between the apron, celestial movements and cosmological beliefs. In Tonga, the heavens are the domain

of the creation god, Tangaloa; it is from them that the god came down to earth to impregnate a woman, a descendant of a worm. The Tu'i Tonga and his descendants wore this apron, and as descendants of the first child, 'Aho'eitu, the spatial arrangement of the materials could therefore have acted to affirm the chiefly lineage's connection to divine power and authority. The *sisi fale* thus appears to carry with it ideas of containment, as not only does it resemble a basket, but it also visually reaffirms that all chiefly lines are somehow encompassed by the connection to the Tu'i Tonga, the apical ancestor whose spatial domain derives directly from the heavens.

## String-Figure Looping

String-figure looping was practised in many Pacific islands, although there is evidence to suggest that the tradition is dying out. In Tonga, string-figure configurations record barkcloth designs, as well as recounting the stories of the gods responsible for the creation of the Tongan islands, their landscape and their people. In a similar fashion to barkcloth, baskets and plaited aprons, string figures rely on an openwork design that acts both as an attention-drawing mechanism and as an anchor for articulating genealogies.

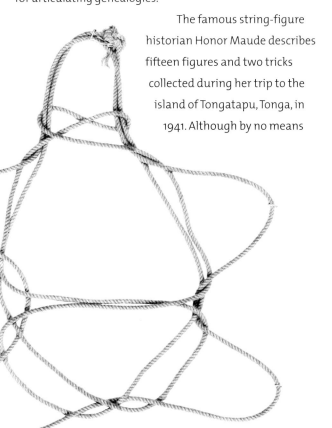

The famous string-figure historian Honor Maude describes fifteen figures and two tricks collected during her trip to the island of Tongatapu, Tonga, in 1941. Although by no means

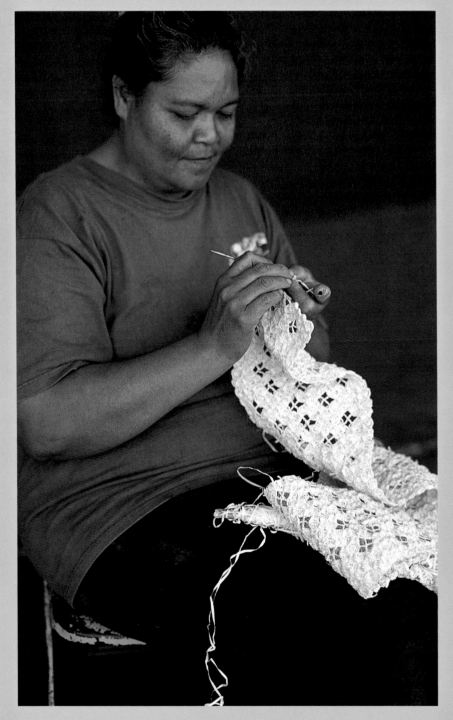

shapes and storytelling in this specific context, though the names of the string figures suggest it is there. For example, many of the names refer to Hina and Sinilau, two Tongan gods. Following Maude's instructions on how to perform the string figures, it appears that the openwork shapes recall the stories of these divine ancestors, enhanced by the spatial forms that resemble key component parts of the myth.

Two string-figure configurations in particular tell the story of the female Hina and her separation from the male god Sinilau. One string figure is titled *Kato 'a Hina*, 'Hina's basket', while the other one is *marae 'a Hina mo Sinilau*, 'the parting of Hina and Sinilau'. The string figures recall the story of Hina, a beautiful moon goddess who was turned into a reef after becoming distraught at her separation from her husband, Sinilau (who may have jumped out of Hina's basket). As a god, he can transform himself from a handsome young man into a terrifying shark with a wide-open mouth, ready to devour his prey.

Two people perform the string figure *Kato 'a Hina*: the first loops the string around his or her wrists and manipulates the index fingers and thumbs so that the string makes a series of parallel lines running between each hand and between opposing fingers; the second person inserts a finger, from below, through the first player's left wrist loop and hooks, downwards, four crossed strings in the centre of the configuration. The first person manipulates the string again by grasping various strands so that the figure resembles a basket shape. The string figure is further manipulated to commence the story of Hina and Sinilau's parting by the second person removing his or her finger, and the first person pulling his or her hands slowly apart.

In another string figure configuration, *aka'i fa* (the name of a barkcloth pattern), Maude describes how the string loop is manipulated with the aid of the foot. A number of hand movements are performed to reveal two diamond figures in the string, suspended between each open hand. These shapes resemble motifs that appear on barkcloth.

## Crochet Work

Victorian needlecrafts introduced into Tonga during the colonial period by the wives of missionaries and French Marist nuns (such as crochet, sewing, embroidery and lace-making) were

a representative sample (as it documents only ten per cent of the string figures then known to be in use), as she acknowledges, her work provides detailed instructions of hand movements accompanied by diagrams of final string-figure configurations. In almost all cases, the string figures are given a name.

In the same manner in which the cat's cradle recounts popular folk stories in Western societies, Tongan string figures actually relate events that occurred in the past, as the hands manipulate the string to form a series of openwork shapes. Maude does not provide evidence of the linkage between string

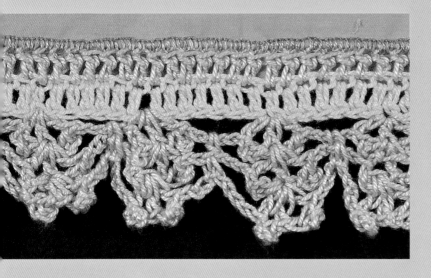

Opposite: Meli Vesi crocheting, Nuku'alofa, Tonga, 2003. Crocheting is an everyday activity for women in Tonga from which they knit waist coverings for men (*ta'ovala*) and women (*kiekie*).

Clockwise from top left: Details of crochetwork, Tonga, 2003; Mele Mafi Tongai knitting regular openwork designs, Nuku'alofa, Tonga, 2003. In crocheting, women are able to create new designs in openwork by altering the number of stitches.

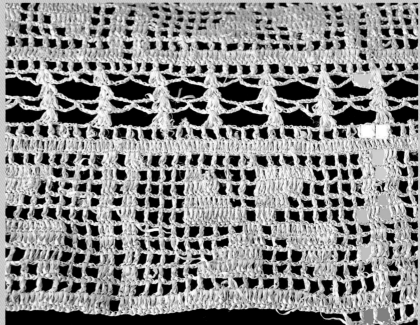

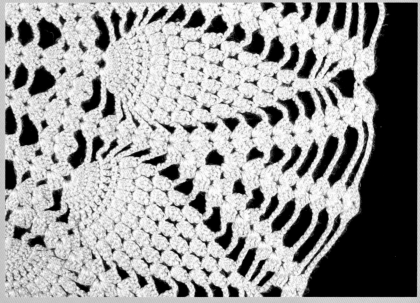

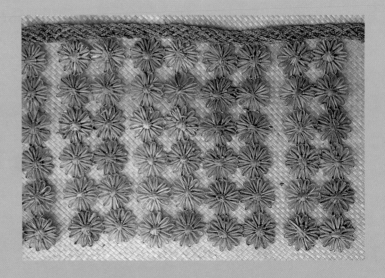

Right: Crocheted women's waist covering, *kiekie*, constructed from the fibrous stem of the hibiscus plant and made by Pase Pa Christmas, Nuku'alofa, Tonga, 2003.

Below: Pase Pa Christmas crochets a *kiekie*, Nuku'alofa, Tonga, 2003.

Opposite, top: Crocheted men's wrapper, *ta'voala*, made from the fibrous stem of the hibiscus plant and worked into openwork patterns, Tonga.

Opposite, centre: *Kiekie* made from dyed hibiscus fibre and translucent white plastic, Tonga.

Opposite, bottom: Women's waist covering, *kiekie*, made from pandanus palm leaf, Tonga.

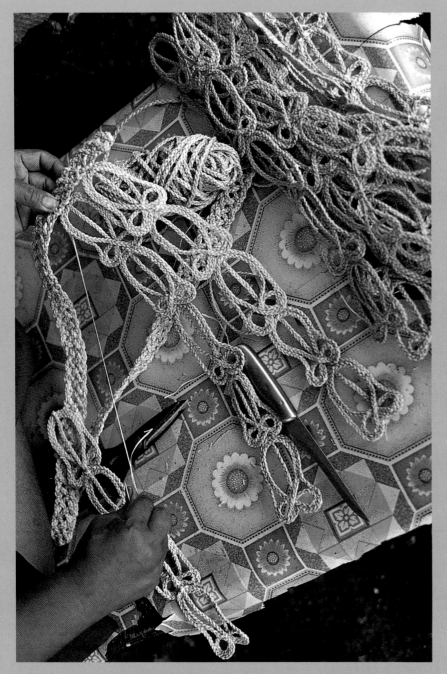

largely responsible for innovations in local fibre arts. They imparted their needlecraft skills to Tongan women in the hope that they would bestow an image more befitting of Victorian femininity. These new techniques, many based on the needle and thread, had a close affinity with pre-existing fibre-art techniques in Tonga – which raises important questions as to why key technologies were adopted in the region. In present-day fibre-based forms we can see how these introduced techniques revolutionized the way women worked, no more so than in innovative uses of crochet work.

Crochet differs from embroidery in that there is no foundation material. However, it originally developed out of a form of chain-stitch embroidery done with a hook instead of a needle, so there is a texture of looped and interlinked chains of thread. Tongan women found they had local fibres ideal for use in crochet. The strength of the fibres of the inner bark of a giant hibiscus tree (*fau*) made them an ideal medium. These fibres are first soaked for two weeks in the sea, which rots away the outer bark while bleaching and softening the inner bark, making it pliable and white. The fibres are removed from the sea, the outer

Overleaf, left: Noble Frederica Lupe'uluiva Fatafeti Lapaha Tuita dressed in girdle, mat, shells and headdress for King Tupou IV's 85th birthday celebration, Nuku'alofa, Tonga, 2003.

Overleaf, right: A range of Tongan clothing worn with *kiekie* and *ta'ovala* at King Tupou IV's 85th birthday celebrations, Nuku'alofa, Tonga, 2003. Clockwise from top left: *Ta'ovala* secured with cord; *kiekie*; Check-patterned *ta'ovala*; *ta'ovala*; *ta'ovala*; *kiekie*.

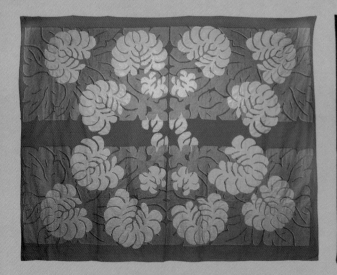

ones being separated and discarded. The remaining inner fibres are washed and left to dry in the sun.

Today, fibre threads are crocheted into mats, overskirts, necklaces and dance decorations. Arguably the most innovative fibre creation involving crochet work is the woman's openwork skirt, the *kiekie*. These openwork overskirts are made from discarded items – such as old cloth, tinsel or recycled flour bags – and hang around a Tongan woman's waist. A number of strips of crocheted fibre, rectangular in shape, hang vertically from a cord tied around a woman's waistline.

*Kiekie* are not normally considered *koloa*: generally, they are not worn at formal occasions and there is a marked lack of investment in their technical production, though ones made from valuable materials such as feathers and pearl shells are indeed considered *koloa*. Although these aprons are not displayed ostentatiously, as a form of wealth, their design (like that of barkcloth, *sisi fale* and string figures) centres on a lattice grid wrapped around the waist. The *kiekie* has the advantage over *ta'ovala* of aiding air circulation and bodily movement: the woven strips hang loose from the waistline so that as the wearer moves, the *kiekie* gently sways. As a contemporary replacement for the *ta'ovala*, the *kiekie* can be worn at church and as part of everyday attire, and plays on new feminine ideals of the body politic and individuality. Unlike Tongan *koloa*, however, *kiekie* resist associations with genealogical relations, as they are quick to make and, as a fashion accessory, have very short lifespans. Yet, in a similar manner to barkcloth, baskets and aprons, *kiekie*, with their crocheted lattice-work designs, carry with them ideas of containment. Women often remark that they cannot leave home without wearing one: in other words, *kiekie* are an essential component of everyday wear, a bound envelope containing the body within.

## Layer and Lattice in the Cook Islands

In eastern Polynesia, by comparison, the destruction of clothed wooden sculptures by members of the London Missionary Society halted the ritual use of barkcloth and fine mats forever. Here, in a move that was as swift as it was unremarkable, techniques of cutting and sewing transformed the work that went into the patterning of layered funerary cloaks made of barkcloth, and into the covering of wooden figures with fine mats and protruding feather holders intricately knotted into the shape of flowers. An efflorescence of pattern innovation – using the ready-made mediums of dress-material and used, cut-up clothing – henceforth shaped the development of *tivaivai* across the Cook Islands, the Hawaiian Islands and Tahiti. Described as 'quilts', *tivaivai* are more accurately 'sewing'. It was the imprinting of designs – through patchwork, embroidery and appliqué techniques, using pre-coloured and pre-patterned material – that led, through the folding and cutting of cloth, to quilt-like garments emulating latticed works.

Nineteenth-century collections highlight a marked contrast between barkcloth from different areas of the Pacific: examples from eastern Polynesia demonstrated a preoccupation with coloration that was distinctly absent in Fiji and Tonga during the same period. Cook Island barkcloth, in particular, came in large, rectangular sheets, some of which were bright yellow on both sides and measured approximately three metres by two – the size of today's *tivaivai*. Other pieces were dark and matt brown on one surface, with a shiny, almost black, appearance on the

other surface, which was overlaid but finely cutout. This form of decoration was achieved by soaking the cloth in the mud of the sago swamp, washing and drying it, and then rubbing the other side with a mixture of grated turmeric and coconut. Flowers and coconut cream were used in perfuming the cloth. The significance of this will become clear when considering the later naturalistic representation of flowers in *tivaivai*. It appears that stitching not only enabled the realization of technical concerns with layering, but also with the metaphorical capture of smell in the use of coloured materials depicting floral imagery.

Today, there are three different types of *tivaivai*. The most characteristic of both Tahiti and the Cook Islands in eastern Polynesia is a piecework design that is sometimes made of up to five thousand rectangular or diamond-shaped pieces which are sewn into eight or twelve triangular sections before being assembled. The same technique of creating patterns by stringing together coloured pieces is used in the Cook Islands to make headbands (designed to fit over hats) from shells. The overall pattern that emerges when the *tivaivai* is assembled is composed of multiple replicated motifs, placed in a complex and often rotating or diagonally offset symmetry. Motifs recall place-making activities such as planting flowers or crops such as pineapple or breadfruit, while anchors, crosses or abstract geometric designs using pre-patterned cloth are seen on *tivaivai* dating from the first half of the twentieth century. Like other type of *tivaivai*, a backing of a distinctive colour, offsetting the foreground, is used and may be repeatedly altered as the *tivaivai* ages. Striking in its use of colour is the second type of *tivaivai*, the appliqué, which is practised mostly in the Cook Islands. Here, multicoloured thread creates a distinctive three-dimensional effect to the surface of replicated floral cut-outs that are superimposed on to a coloured background, again in a striking symmetrical fashion. The third type of *tivaivai*, known as 'snowflake' or 'cut-out' design, amplifies the disorientating effect of manipulating visually, through coloured pattern, the relation between foreground and background in that, at its best, the eye finds it hard to see which of the two colours composes the surface pattern.

The coloured pattern of the *tivaivai* appears both to absorb and reflect light, reminding one of the black and luminous pearls found in this part of the Pacific. Great care is taken in the cutting and sewing of the *tivaivai* to create a symmetry that works as

remembered and passed on from one generation to another. The importance assigned to *tivaivai* in the history of a household may explain the fact that, although *tivaivai* are big enough to fit a double bed, they tend not to be used as a decorative cover, but are kept folded up in treasure trunks to emerge only at significant life-cycle rituals when they are gifted often repeatedly, only finally to disappear from view forever when they are wrapped around the dead.

*Tivaivai* anchor genealogy, and allow for it to be seen as a path of intersecting connections through which one can trace back from a picture of many people to a picture of one apical ancestor. Genealogies are staggeringly long in the Cook Islands as elsewhere in eastern Polynesia, and it is not uncommon for many generations to be counted back to a founding ancestor. Such recitations of genealogical connections coincide with the public gifting of a *tivaivai* at a wedding or funeral, when those who receive the *tivaivai* become part of a mnemonic system of places and paths recalled through the symmetrically arranged motifs and tracks that cover the *tivaivai*.

The site for anchoring genealogical powers is the house, a fact that has allowed *tivaivai* to reconcile ideas of spatio-temporal transformation of the one and the many with the notions of domesticity and time-keeping that were popularized with Christianity. So it is that in the Cook Island graves are still erected in house-like structures at the entrance to the residence, and are filled with quilt-like garments that wrap the body at death. Surrounded by a floral garden, the grave should be visible from the doorway and veranda of the residence, where women sit and sew on a daily basis.

While the sewing of the *tivaivai* is a solitary activity, there are usually several women involved in the production of a single quilt: one may have drawn and cut the design from cloth, and another may have embroidered and stitched the cut-out design on to a rectangular sheet of cloth, while other more complicated quilts may involve the cooperation of up to eight women working together to complete a quilt. Women tend to sew *tivaivai* for regular competitive displays organized by the church they attend.

Most women have their own collections of *tivaivai* that are kept hidden in a box. They consist, in part, of their own *tivaivai*, most if not all of which have already been given away, but which are kept in care for their sons and daughters while they lead busy

much in terms of its spatial and formal arrangement as in its colour. This is done by multiplying a single chosen motif, which is itself a composite of different-coloured cloth pieces, and arranging the thus replicated motif symmetrically on the surface of a coloured sheet of cloth. The pattern of the *tivaivai* is thus fractal in its spatial composition, as the overall composite pattern can be reduced to a singular elemental motif.

It is perhaps this fractal property of pattern in the *tivaivai* that has enabled the quilts to serve as genealogical markers , allowing family connections that sustain a household to be

working lives abroad. Other items in the collections are given at major gifting occasions, usually at any son's first haircut, children's twenty-first birthdays, weddings and funerals. Among the women who are known to be members of a sewing group, only one or two are generally responsible for designing and cutting the pattern, irrespective of what type of *tivaivai* is to be made. In return, they will either be recompensed by the group for their work or receive help with their own stitching.

One may wonder why there are three distinct types of *tivaivai*. To suggest that the distinct designs, from proper

Preceding pages: Hand-painted *tivaivai* displayed at the Seventh Day Adventist Exhibition, Titikaveka, Rarotonga, Cook Islands, 2003. The hand-painting of the *tivaivai*, using stencils made from lino, was recently introduced into the islands by expatriate Cook Islanders living in Auckland, New Zealand.

Opposite: *Tivaivai* made in Rakahanga, northern Cook Islands,

1991. The *tivaivai* design is cut out and embroidered using cloth bought from local stores.

Above: Tokerau Munro and Vereara Maeva stitch a cut-out *tivaivai* design on to its cloth backing. Women's groups centred around local churches focus their efforts on the competitive sewing and display of *tivaivai*, Arorangi, Rarotonga, Cook Islands, 2003.

'patchwork' to appliqué and cutout, would correspond to distinctions that are observed in social relations or even to stages in the life of an individual would be wrong. In the same way as it is not possible to say that specific patterns are chosen for specific purposes or to signal the relation a woman may have with the person for whom she is making the *tivaivai*, so it is not possible to pin patterns down to individual owners. Instead, it would be more accurate to think of designs as visually recalling acts of patterning, such as cutting, threading and stitching. The designs are the starting point for conceiving an attachment that is formed and secured repeatedly by making present a significant, but absent, entity – a person, a place or a thing that is encompassed within and yet can be activated only in the mind. The question of how background can become foreground is solved visually and geometrically in *tivaivai* in ways that are performatively and rhythmically acted out in dance, music, poetry, and surely, in times gone by, in ritual. *Tivaivai* are thus as much about the choreography of dance movement, itself falling into three types

(action, drum and chant), and the composition of hymn, song and speech, as they are about a genealogical theory of mind.

To understand how patterning in *tivaivai* reflects upon acts of social remembering, it is useful to look at the three types of *tivaivai* in greater detail. Firstly, there is the patchwork (*taorei*), the possession of which embeds the maker and the current owner of the *tivaivai* in a continuous succession of entitlement. Significantly, the patterns of such patchworks recall certain places, the most important of which is a lineage's *marai* or ceremonial ground, knowledge of which sanctions the use of land across generations. Such *tivaivai* also feature the most fractal and abstract type of pattern, which is remembered not by what it represents, but by a sequence of numbers represented by coloured patches. When flowers are represented at all in such patterns, they are often depicted from an unusual perspective, obfuscating normal visual recognition. Patchworks of this kind recall the painted *moenga* or sleeping mats that are still used today to work out the design. The pattern, always consisting of multiple replicated motifs (*pu*) connected by trails (*tarere*), is recalled as a numbered series of coloured pieces, which are threaded in exact number and sequence on to a string. This string of coloured pieces is then sewn into eight or twelve triangular pieces of cloth, with the women calling out the number of coloured pieces to be sewn, in turn, before the entire *tivaivai* is assembled and the overall pattern becomes apparent. Individual triangles can be kept and used as a template for re-creating similar pieces when the *tivaivai* has been taken off its backing and has begun to disintegrate. Women recall their friendships or familial ties by referring to these patchworks, which are treasured by generations. *Taorei* are personal possessions that, if they are not wrapped around the owner

at death, are gifted as a token of succession – usually to a favourite grandchild.

Secondly, there is the appliqué *tivaivai* (*ta taura*) most commonly produced in the Cook Islands, whose gifting marks the setting-up of new households at marriage, and thus the branching of the lineage into multiple, intersecting clans. The patterns of such appliqué *tivaivai* feature a distinctive play on the mathematical constraints of plane-symmetry, as flowers are arranged in a precise, often rotating or diagonally offset, mirror-like manner. Topologically such *tivaivai* recall the three-dimensionality of the planar surface, a fact which is enhanced by the detailed embroidery that gives depth to depicted flowers in an often hyper-real manner. Like the hand gestures of a dancer or the geometric positioning of a dance group, the rotational movement of the stitched appliqué outlines a theme that is well known and generic, one that touches the heart of everyone who cares to see and to listen: stories of love and of loss talk about experiences which resonate, often against all the odds, in the here and now.

Finally, there is the cut-out (*manu*) *tivaivai* that marks the most impermanent of all connections. Its distinctive two-dimensional frame, whose foreground and background appear to fuse together, is the result of a process of folding and cutting fibrous material to create a symmetrically repeated design across a plane. If possible, one should cut out the design so finely that, when superimposed upon a material of a different colour, the cut-out appears to recede against part of the background. Quick to make and easy to give away, this type of *tivaivai* condenses time quite literally into a moment. During the tacking down of the cut-out material, women sit in the centre of the fabric, reminiscent of the stencilling and freehand drawing of barkcloth in other parts of the Pacific.

Similarities with barkcloth production are even more striking in a recent innovation in the creation of quilts. In some parts of the Cook Islands, competitive church-based displays of quilts have begun to feature the painting rather than the sewing of *tivaivai*. This innovation was developed by an Auckland-based Cook Island community and is considered appealing as it enables the rapid production of large quantities of patterned fabric compared to conventional sewing methods. Designing painted *tivaivai* involves cutting motifs out of linoleum flooring into stencils, usually in the shape of flowers around which outlines are traced on to sheets of cloth. The stencilled motifs are then coloured through freehand drawing by women who work in large groups to complete the quilts. Noticeable is the large size of both the finished product and the stencilled patterns.

As large and as visually dominant as *tivaivai* are when exhibited – in what amounts to almost an 'ideal home exhibition' setting – they are not usually displayed in the house, and are folded up and hidden from view for most of their existence. *Tivaivai* are paradoxically a thing of the mind, for as *tivaivai* patterns are remade several times in a maker's lifetime, they

recall both personal and biographical history such as the birth of a child or friendships struck in the workplace, as well as enabling others who inherit a quilt from a grandmother or mother to internalize genealogical connections as their own.

Although these two case studies centre on Polynesian fibre arts, they illustrate the manifest ways pattern captures temporal and spatial modes of situating oneself in the world that can be generalized across the Pacific. Pattern carries with it the ability to traverse cultural boundaries through its translatability from artefact to performance to architectural space to social histories

and back to artefact again. Pattern becomes reproducible through memory, being inscribed in gestural and rhythmic movements, and with its notational quality being akin to music, dance and number. As such, pattern is not a matter of the physical body alone, but a tangible trace of the mind transposed across analogical domains as it is performed and textured. Yet we must be wary of thinking of pattern as a static and immutable entity which is merely visual or audible. Pacific pattern comes into its own as efficacious action: it guides the fashioning of cloth and fibre threads into the latest dress designs as much as it inspires

the many ways of wrapping the body or designing architectural space. The surfaces fashioned by pattern in the Pacific are far from superficial and superfluous, as the often ephemeral material may lead us to believe. Pacific pattern is profound because it is both the cause and the effect of action, revealing a dynamic that intimately interlinks the mental with the material conditions for life. This story of pattern in the Pacific – plaited and bound in fibre and fabric – shows how the most everyday of things carries forward the most profound of ideas in the most subtle of ways.

Page 194: Appliqué *tivaivai* displayed on a bed in the home of the Queen of Arorangi, Arorangi, Cook Islands, 1998.

Page 195, left: Tepaeru Teao making *tivaivai* pillowcases from a cut-out design in Otara, Auckland, New Zealand, 2004.

Page 195, right: Women sit together cutting and sewing a *tivaivai* in Otara, Auckland, New Zealand, 2004.

Preceding pages: *Tivaivai* on exhibition at the Seventh Day Adventist Church, Titikaveka, Rarotonga, Cook Islands, 2003. Church exhibitions are organized by the local priest's wife, and there are competitive events with prizes presented to the winner of the best *tivaivai* design. *Tivaivai* are usually

kept in treasure boxes and are only displayed at the annual open-house event or at competitive exhibitions. From left to right: Appliqué *tivaivai* displayed with pillows on settee; appliqué *tivaivai* displayed with pillows on bed against lace curtains.

Above and opposite: In eastern Polynesia, the destruction of clothed wooden sculptures by members of the London Missionary Society halted the ritual use of barkcloth and fine mats forever. New sewing technologies led to an efflorescence of pattern, using the ready-made media of dress material and used, cut-up clothing. This shaped the development of *tivaivai* across the Cook, Hawaiian and Society Islands. These details of *tivaivai* were made by Mrs Akaiti Ama, Rarotonga, Cook Islands.

Clockwise, from left to right: 'Ideal home exhibition' of *tivaivai* with painted mats, tablecloths and furniture at the Seventh Day Adventist Exhibition, Titikaveka, Rarotonga, Cook Islands, 2003; detail of appliqué *tivaivai* displayed at the Seventh Day Adventist Exhibition, Titikaveka, Rarotonga, Cook Islands, 2003; appliqué *tivaivai* hand sewn and embroidered with 'matirita' chrysanthemum flower designs in a complex symmetrical pattern, made by Emily Puni, Teariki Rakei of Atiu, Cook Islands, in 1998 and first shown in a local competition in 2001.

NORTH PACIFIC OCEAN

MICRONESIA

PALAU
·

CAROLINE ISLANDS

MARSHALL ISLANDS

·Pohnpei

New Ireland

KIRIBATI

IRIAN JAYA   Sepik

Bougainville

TOKELAU

·Mount Hagen

SOLOMON
ISLANDS

PAPUA NEW GUINEA

TUVALU

·Port Moresby

MELANESIA

SAMOA

VANUATU

WALLIS
AND FUTUNA

FIJI
ISLANDS

NIUE

TONGA

NEW
CALEDONIA

AUSTRALIA

POLYNESIA

North Island

NEW ZEALAND

TASMANIA

South Island

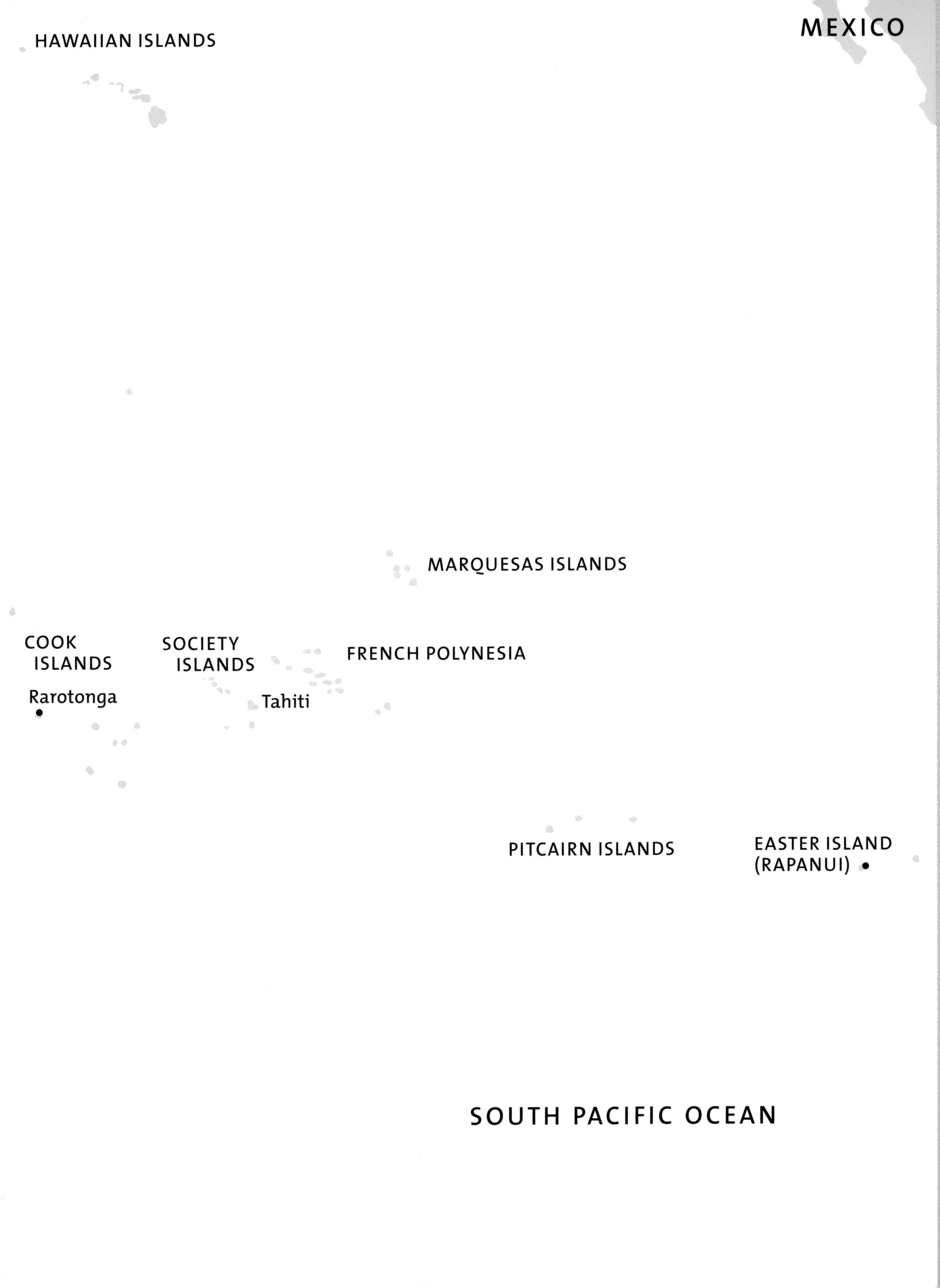

HAWAIIAN ISLANDS

MEXICO

MARQUESAS ISLANDS

COOK
ISLANDS

SOCIETY
ISLANDS

FRENCH POLYNESIA

Rarotonga

Tahiti

PITCAIRN ISLANDS

EASTER ISLAND
(RAPANUI)

SOUTH PACIFIC OCEAN

# BIBLIOGRAPHY

## INTRODUCTION

Arbeit, Wendy. *What are Fronds For?* Honolulu, Hawaii: University of Hawaii Press, 1985.

Boas, Franz. *Primitive Art.* Cambridge, Mass.: Harvard University Press and Oslo: H. Aschelong and Co., 1927.

Brookfield, H. C. with Doreen Hart. *Melanesia: A Geographical Interpretation of an Island World.* London: Methuen, 1971.

D'Alleva, Anne. *Art of the Pacific.* London: Weidenfeld and Nicolson, 1998.

Forge, Anthony, ed. *Primitive Art and Society.* New York: Oxford University Press, 1973.

Forty, Adrian. *Objects of Desire: Design and Society, 1750–1980.* London: Thames & Hudson, 1986.

Gathercole, Peter, Adrienne L. Kaeppler and Douglas Newton. *The Art of the Pacific Islands.* Washington, D.C.: National Gallery of Art, 1979.

Gombrich, Ernst. *The Sense of Order: A Study in the Psychology of Decorative Art.* Oxford: Phaidon, 1984.

Hanson, Allen and Louise Hanson, eds. *Art and Identity in Oceania.* Honolulu: University of Hawaii Press, 1990.

Ingold, Tim. 'Making Culture and Weaving the World' in P. M. Graves-Brown, ed., *Matter, Materiality and Modern Culture.* London and New York: Routledge, 2000.

Ingold, Tim. *The Perception of the Environment: Essays on Livelihood, Dwelling and Skill.* London and New York: Routledge, 2000.

Jewell, Rebecca and Jude Lloyd. *Pacific Designs.* London: British Museum Press, 1998.

Kirch, Patrick. *The Lapita Peoples: Ancestors of the Oceanic World.* Cambridge, Mass.: Blackwell Publishers, 1997.

Mead, Sydney M., ed. *Exploring the Visual Arts of Oceania: Australia, Melanesia, Micronesia*

*and Polynesia.* Honolulu: University of Hawaii Press, 1979.

Riegl, Alois. *Problems of Style: Foundations for a History of Ornament.* Princeton, NJ: Princeton University Press, 1992. First published in Germany, 1893.

Schuster, C. and Edmund Carpenter. *Patterns that Connect: Social Symbolism in Ancient and Tribal Art.* New York: Harry N. Abrams, 1996.

Smith, Bernard. *European Vision and the South Pacific.* Second edition. New Haven: Yale University Press, 1985.

Thomas, Nicholas. *Oceanic Art.* London and New York: Thames & Hudson, 1995.

— *Entangled Objects: Exchange, Material Culture, and Colonialism in the Pacific.* Cambridge, Mass.: Harvard University Press, 1991.

Trilling, James. *The Language of Ornament.* London and New York: Thames & Hudson, 2001.

Washburn, Dorothy Koster and Donald W. Crowe. *Symmetries of Culture: Theory and Practice of Plane Pattern Analysis.* Seattle: University of Washington Press, 1988.

## A HISTORY OF PATTERN IN FIBRE AND FABRIC IN THE SOUTH PACIFIC

Arbeit, Wendy. *Baskets in Polynesia.* With photographs by Douglas Peebles. Honolulu: University of Hawaii Press, 1990.

Biskop, P. *Memoires of Dampier.* Pacific History Series. Canberra: Australian National University Press, 1975.

Boutilier, J., D. Hughes and S. Tiffany. *Mission, Church, and Sect in Oceania.* ASAO Monograph 6. Lanham, MD: University Press of America, 1978.

Brown, George. *Pioneer Missionary and Explorer: An Autobiography. A Narrative of Forty-eight Years' Residence and Travel in Samoa, New Britain, New Ireland, New Guinea and the Solomon Islands.* London: Hodder & Stoughton, 1908.

Colchester, Chloe, ed. *Clothing the Pacific.* Oxford: Berg, 2003.

Crocombe, Ronald G. *The New South Pacific.* Canberra: Australian National University Press, 1973.

Defert, Daniel. 'The Collection of the World: Accounts of Voyages from the Sixteenth to the Eighteenth Centuries' in *Dialectical Anthropology 7*, No. 1 (September 1982).

Dunmore, John. *French Explorers in the Pacific.* 2 volumes. Oxford: Clarendon Press, 1965.

Elsner, John and Roger Cardinal, eds. *The Cultures of Collecting.* Cambridge, Mass.: Harvard University Press, 1994.

Evans, Joan. *Pattern: A Study of Ornament in Western Europe from 1180 to 1900.* Oxford: Clarendon Press, 1931, and New York: Da Capo Press, 1976.

Finsch, Otto. *Samoa Fahrten. Reisen im Kaiser Wilhelmland und Englisch Neuguinea, 1884–1885.* Berlin: Heineman, 1914.

Forster, Georg. *Werke in vier Bänden.* Frankfurt a.M.: Insel-Verlag, 1967–1970. Introduced by Gerhard Steiner.

Greenblatt, Stephen Jay. *Marvelous Possessions: The Wonder of the New World.* Chicago: University of Chicago Press, 1991.

Haddon, Alfred C. *Evolution in Art: As Illustrated by the Life-Histories of Designs.* London: Walter Scott, 1895, and New York: AMS Press, 1979.

Hooper, Steven. 'Memorial Images of Eastern Fiji: Materials, Metaphors and Allusion' in Anita Herle et al, eds, *Pacific Art: Persistence, Change, and Meaning.* Adelaide: Crawford House and Honolulu: University of Hawaii Press, 2002.

Howe, K. R., Robert C. Kiste and Brij V. Lal, eds. *Tides of History: The Pacific Islands in the Twentieth Century.* Australia, NSW: Allen & Unwin Ltd and Honolulu: University of Hawaii Press, 1994.

Jones, Owen. *The Grammar of Ornament.* New York: Van Nostrand Reinhold Co., 1972. First published in 1856.

Kaeppler, Adrienne L. *'Artificial Curiosities': being an exposition of native manufacturers collected on the three Pacific voyages of Captain James Cook, R.N., at the Bernice Pauahi Bishop Museum, January 18, 1978 – August 31, 1978, on the occasion of the bicentennial of the European discovery of the Hawaiian Islands by Captain Cook.* Honolulu: Bishop Museum Press, 1978.

—, ed. *Cook Voyage Artifacts in Leningrad, Berne, and Florence Museums.* Honolulu: Bishop Museum Press, 1978.

— 'L'Art Oceanien' in *Art et grandes civilisations*, 23. Paris: Citadelles & Mazenod, 1993.

— *Pacific Island and Australian Aboriginal Artifacts in Public Collections in the United States of America and Canada.* Paris: United Nations Educational Scientific Cultural Organization, 1985.

— 'Pacific Festivals and the Promotion of Identity, Politics, and Tourism' in *Come mek me hol' yu han'.* Jamaica: Jamaica Memory Bank, 1988.

Langdon, Robert. 'New World Cotton as a Clue to the Polynesian Past' in Jukka Siikala, ed., *Transactions of the Finnish Anthropological Society II.* Juonen Antropologinen Seura, 1982.

O'Hanlon, Michael and Robert L. Welsch, eds. *Hunting the Gatherers: Ethnographic Collectors, Agents and Agency in Melanesia, 1870s–1930s.* New York and Oxford: Berghahn Books, 2000.

Otto, Ton and Ad Borsboom. *Cultural Dynamics of Religious Change in Oceania.* Leiden, Netherlands: KITLV Press, 1997.

Strathern, Marilyn. 'Artefacts of History: Events and the Interpretation of Images' in Jukka Siikala, ed., *Culture and History in the Pacific.* Helsinki: Finnish Anthropological Society, 1990.

Sturma, Michael. 'Dressing, Undressing and Early European Contact in Australia and Tahiti' in *Pacific Studies*, Vol. 21 (3).

Thomas, Nicholas. 'Licensed Curiosity. Cook's Pacific Voyages' in John Elsner and Roger Cardinal, eds, *The Cultures of Collecting.* Cambridge, Mass.: Harvard University Press, 1994.

Were, Graeme. *Pattern, Thought and the Construction of Knowledge: The Question of the Kapkap from New Ireland, Papua New Guinea.* Unpublished PhD Dissertation, University of London, 2003.